My Book

This book belongs to

Name: ______________________________

MK
MATH
KNOTS
Joy of Learning....

Cover Design by :
Gowri Vemuri

First Edition :
December , 2019

Author :
Gowri Vemuri

Edited by :
Ritvik Pothapragada
Siddhartha Rangavajjula

Questions: mathknots.help@gmail.com

NOTE : ACSL is neither affiliated nor sponsors or endorses this product.

MK
MATH
KNOTS
Joy of Learning...

Dedication

This book is dedicated to:

My Mom, who is my best critic, guide and supporter.

To what I am today, and what I am going to become tomorrow,

is all because of your blessings, unconditional affection and support.

This book is dedicated to the

strongest women of my life ,

my dearest mom

and

to all those moms in this universe.

G.V.

MK
MATH
KNOTS
Joy of Learning....

American Computer Science League (ACSL) is an international computer science competition originally founded in 1978. This organization is also an institutional member of the Computer Science Teachers Association. ACSL is on the approved activities list of the National Association of Secondary School Principals (NASSP).

ACSL consists of five divisions to appeal to the varying computing abilities and interests of students. All students at a school can take the tests but can only participate in one division. A team score is the sum of the best 3 or 5 scores in each test. Those scores can come from different students with in the team, in each contest. Prizes are awarded to top scoring students and teams based on cumulative scores after the 4th test.

The **Senior / Intermediate Division** is geared to those high school students with programming experience. Each contest consists of a 30-minute, 5- questions short answer test and a take home programming problem to be solved in 72-hours. Team scores can be based on the sum of the top 3 or top 5 scores each contest.

The **Junior Division** is geared to junior high and middle school students with no previous experience programming computers. No student beyond grade 9 may compete in the Junior Division. Each contest consists of a 30-minute 5-question short answer test and a take home program to be solved in 72-hours. Team scores are based on the sum of the best 5 scores each test.

The **Classroom Division** is open to students from all grades. It consists of a selection of the non-programming problems. As its name implies, this division is particularly well-suited for use in the classroom. Each contest consists of a 50-minute, 10-question short answer test. Team scores are based on the sum of the best 5 scores each test.
The **Elementary Division** is open to students from grades 3 - 6. It consists of non-programming problems. Four categories, one each contest, will be tested. The contest consists of a 30-minute, 5-questions test.

ELEMENTARY DIVISION	CLASS ROOM / JUNIOR DIVISION	INTERMEDIATE / SENIOR DIVISI
Elementary Computer Number Systems	Computer Number Systems	Computer Number Systems
Elementary Prefix/Infix/Postfix Notation	Recursive Functions	Recursive Functions
Elementary Boolean Algebra	What Does This Program Do? Branching	What Does This Program Do?
Elementary Graph Theory	Prefix/Infix/Postfix Notation	Prefix/Infix/Postfix Notation
	Bit-String Flicking	Bit-String Flicking
	What Does This Program Do? Loops	LISP
	Boolean Algebra	Boolean Algebra
	Data Structures	Data Structures
	What Does This Program Do? Arrays	FSA/Regular Expressions
	Graph Theory	Graph Theory
	Digital Electronics	Digital Electronics
	What Does This Program Do? Strings	Assembly Language

This book is written by computer science teachers and industry experts. Our book comprises of various practice questions in line with ACSL topics.

NOTE: ACSL is neither affiliated nor endorsed the content of this book.

This book is intended to give a hands on practice on various topics covering contest 1 and contest 2.
The questions might not replicate 100% of the actual test but are intended to reinforce the basic concepts.

Boolean Algebra

Boolean Algebra is the mathematics we use to analyze digital gates and circuits. We can use these "Laws of Boolean" to both reduce and simplify a complex Boolean expression in an attempt to reduce the number of logic gates required.
Boolean Algebra is a system of mathematics based on logic that has its own set of rules or laws which are used to define and reduce Boolean expressions.
The variables used in **Boolean Algebra** only have one of two possible values, 0" and "1" but an expression can have an infinite number of variables.
Each variable can have a value of 1 or 0 only.

Laws of Boolean Algebra :

1. Annulment Law – A term AND´ed with a "0" equals 0 or OR´ed with a "1" will equal 1

→ A . 0 = 0 A variable AND'ed with 0 is always equal to 0
→ A + 1 = 1 A variable OR'ed with 1 is always equal to 1

2. Identity Law – A term OR´ed with a "0" or AND´ed with a "1" will always equal that term

→ $A + A = A$
→ $A A = A$
→ A + 0 = A A variable OR'ed with 0 is always equal to the variable
→ A . 1 = A A variable AND'ed with 1 is always equal to the variable

3. Idempotent Law – An input that is AND´ed or OR´ed with itself is equal to that input

→ A + A = A A variable OR'ed with itself is always equal to the variable
→ A . A = A A variable AND'ed with itself is always equal to the variable

4. Complement Law – A term AND´ed with its complement equals "0" and a term OR´ed with its complement equals "1"

→ $\overline{A} . A = 0$ A variable AND'ed with its complement is always equal to 0
→ $\overline{A} + A = 1$ A variable OR'ed with its complement is always equal to 1

5. Commutative Law – The order of application of two separate terms is not important

→ $A . B = B . A$ The order in which two variables are AND'ed makes no difference

→ $A + B = B + A$ The order in which two variables are OR'ed makes no difference

6. Double Negation Law – A term that is inverted twice is equal to the original term

→ $A = A$ A double complement of a variable is always equal to the variable

7. de Morgan´s Theorem – There are two "de Morgan´s" rules or theorems,

→ Two separate terms NOR´ed together is the same as the two terms inverted (Complement) and AND´ed for example: $A+B = A . B$

8. **De Morgan's Theorem**

$\overline{(A + B)} = \bar{A}\,\bar{B}$

→ Two separate terms NAND′ed together is the same as the two terms inverted (Complement) and OR′ed for example: A.B = A + B

$\bar{A}\,\bar{B} = \overline{(A + B)}$

Other algebraic Laws of Boolean not detailed above include:

9. <u>Distributive Law</u> – This law permits the multiplying or factoring out of an expression.

→ A(B + C) = A.B + A.C (OR Distributive Law)
→ A + (B.C) = (A + B).(A + C) (AND Distributive Law)

10. <u>Absorptive Law</u> – This law enables a reduction in a complicated expression to a simpler one by absorbing like terms.

→ A + (A.B) = A (OR Absorption Law)
→ A(A + B) = A (AND Absorption Law)

11. <u>Associative Law</u> – This law allows the removal of brackets from an expression and regrouping of the variables.

→ A + (B + C) = (A + B) + C = A + B + C (OR Associate Law)
→ A(B.C) = (A.B)C = A . B . C (AND Associate Law)

12. $AB + A\overline{B} = A$
    $(A + B)(A + \overline{B}) = A$

13. $A + AB = A$
    $A(A + B) = A$

14. $A + \overline{A}B = (A + B)$

    $A(\overline{A} + B) = AB$

15. $A \oplus B = A\overline{B} + \overline{A}B$
    The *xor* of two values is true whenever the values are different. It uses the $\oplus$ operator, and can be built from the basic operators:

    $A \oplus B = A\overline{B} + \overline{A}B$
    The values of *xor* for all possible inputs are shown in the truth table below

A	B	$A \oplus B$
0	0	0
0	1	1
1	0	1
1	1	0

16. The *xnor* of two values is true whenever the values are the same. It is the *not* of the *xor* function. It uses the $\odot$ operator: $A \odot B = \overline{A \oplus B}$
The *xnor* can be built from basic operators:
$A \odot B = \overline{A \oplus B} = AB + \overline{A}\,\overline{B}$
The values of *xnor* for all possible inputs is shown in the truth table below:

A	B	$A \odot B$
0	0	1
0	1	0
1	0	0
1	1	1

Example :
Simplify the following expression: (A + B)(A + C)

(A + B)(A + C) = A.A + A.C + A.B + B.C (Distributive law)

= A + A.C + A.B + B.C (Idempotent AND Law)

= A(1 + C) + A.B + B.C (Distributive law)

= A.1 + A.B + B.C (Identity OR law)

= A(1 + B) + B.C (Distributive law)

= A + B.C (Identity AND law)

(A + B)(A + C) = A + B.C

Digital Electronics

BUFFER

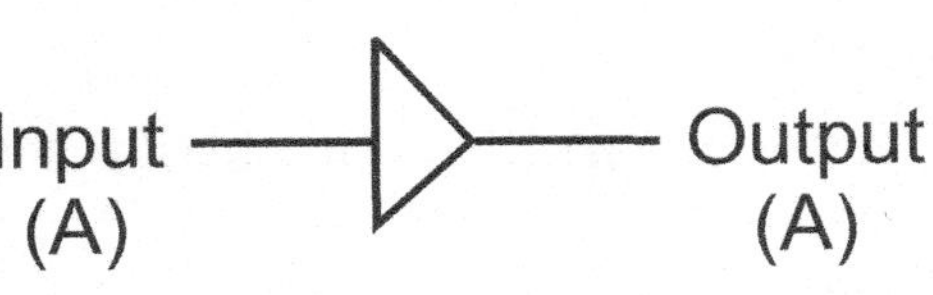

Input	Output
0	0
1	1

NOT

Input (A) → Output (A)

Input	Output
0	1
1	0

AND

Input (A), Input (B) → Output (A)

Input (A)	Input (B)	Output
0	0	0
0	1	0
1	0	0
1	1	1

NAND

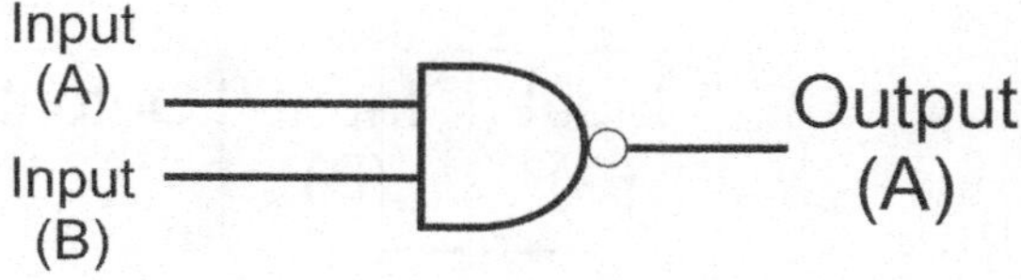

Input (A)	Input (B)	Output
0	0	1
0	1	1
1	0	1
1	1	0

OR

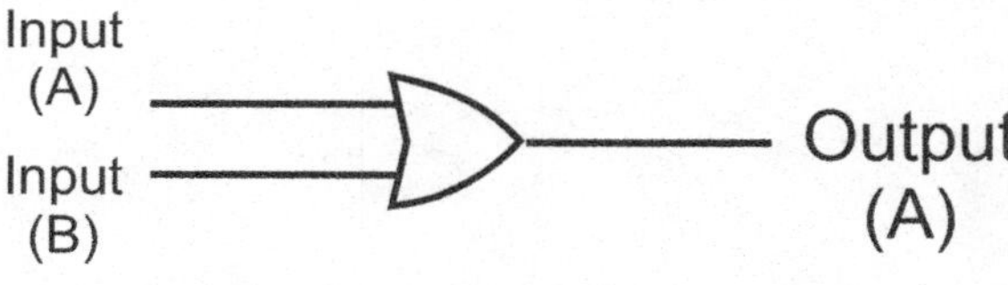

Input (A)	Input (B)	Output
0	0	0
0	1	1
1	0	1
1	1	1

NOR

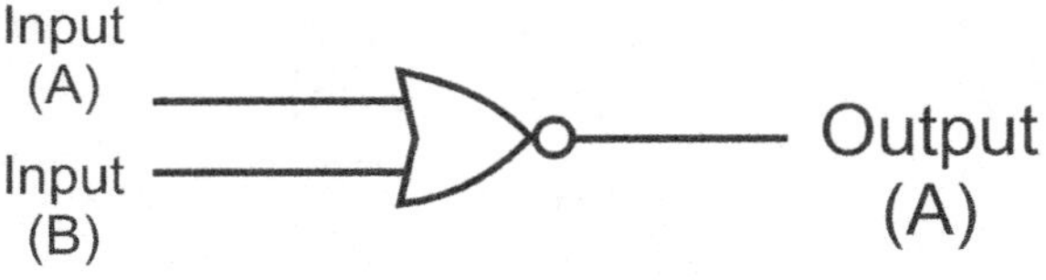

Input (A)	Input (B)	Output
0	0	1
0	1	0
1	0	0
1	1	0

XOR

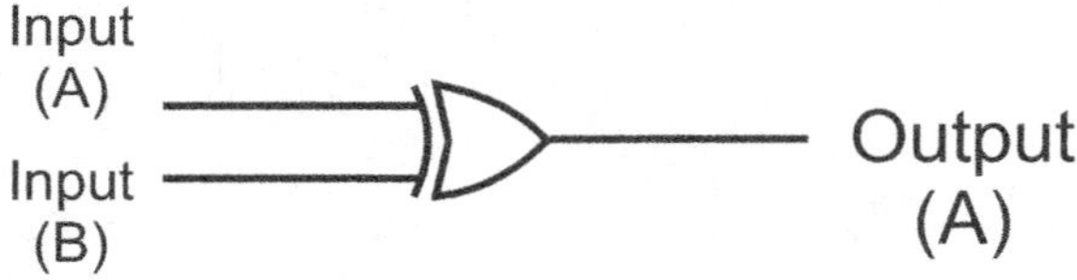

Input (A)	Input (B)	Output
0	0	0
0	1	1
1	0	1
1	1	0

XNOR

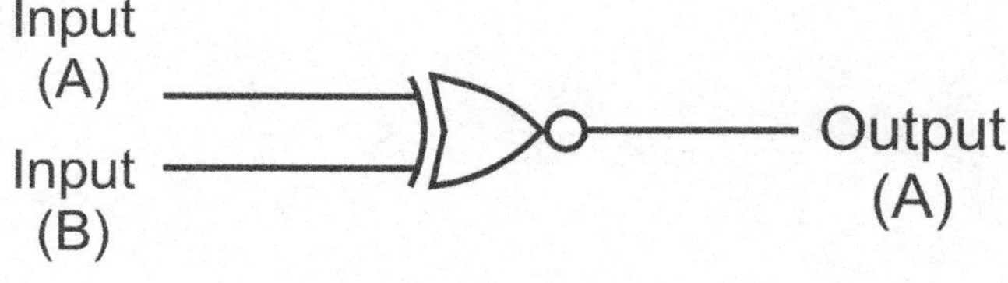

Input (A)	Input (B)	Output
0	0	1
0	1	0
1	0	0
1	1	1

Check www.wixtest.acsl.org/categories
for details on

⟶ Data Structures

⟶ What does this program do ? - Arrays

⟶ Graph Theory

⟶ What does this program do ? - Strings

Boolean Algebra

1. Simplify $C + \overline{BC}$

2. *Simplify* $\overline{AC}(\bar{A} + C)(\bar{C} + C)$

3. *Simplify* $(A + B)(AD + A\overline{D}) + B$

4. Find A OR (A AND B) where A is 011101 and B is 101000.

5. Find B AND (A OR (A AND B)) where A is 0101000 and B is 1110101.

6. Find (A OR B) OR (A AND B) where A is 0111100 and B is 1110101.

7. Prove the commutative law if A is 0101000 and B is 1110001.

8. Find A AND (A OR (A OR B)) if A is 0101000 and B is 1110001.

9 Find C OR (C AND (A AND B)) if A is 01100111 B is 11001101 and C is 01100100

10. Find A OR (A AND (A AND B)) if A is 01100111 and B is 11001101.

11. Prove the associative law if A = 10000111, B is 11001101 and C is 01100100.

12. *Simplify*

$$(A + (B + \bar{B}) + \bar{A}) + \bar{\bar{A}}$$

13. *Simplify*

$$((A(B+\overline{B}))(A+\bar{A}))+\bar{\bar{A}}$$

14. *Prove that* $(AA+\bar{A})\bar{A}+\overline{B}=\overline{AB}$

15. $Simplify$ $(A + A)\bar{A} + (\bar{A} + A)A$

16. $Simplify$ $((A(B + NOT\ B))(A + NOT\ A))$

17. *Prove the following*: $(NOT\ A + (A + F)) = B + \overline{B}$

18. *Simplify* $(A + \overline{B})(A + B) + (A\overline{A})$

19. $Prove\ the\ following, ((A\ OR\ B)\ OR\ (A\ AND\ B))AND\ (A\ AND\ B) = B, where\ A = True\ and\ B\ is\ False$

20. $Prove\ the\ following, ((A\ OR\ A)\ AND\ (B\ AND\ B))\ OR\ (A\ AND\ B) = NOT\quad , where\ A = False\ and\ B\ is\ True$

21. Find A OR NOT (A AND B) if A is TTTFF and B is FFFTT
where T represents True and F represents False

22. Find (A OR B) AND (A OR NOT B)
where A is TFTFFFT and B is FTFFTFF

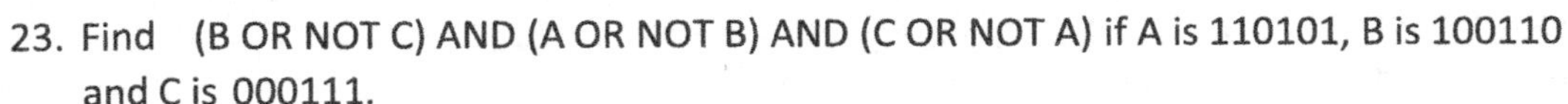

23. Find (B OR NOT C) AND (A OR NOT B) AND (C OR NOT A) if A is 110101, B is 100110 and C is 000111.

24. Find (A OR NOT B) OR (C OR NOT NOT A) if A is 100101, B is 100110 and C is 000111.

25. Find (A OR NOT NOT B) OR (C OR NOT NOT A) AND (A AND B)
    if A is 000101, B is 100100, C is 100101.

26. Find (A OR C) OR (C AND A) AND (A AND B) if A is TTFFT, B is FFTTT and C is TTTTF

27. Find (A AND C) OR (C AND NOT C) AND (A AND NOT NOT A) A= TFFFT, C= TFTFF

28. *Prove that*

$$((A(B+\bar{B}))(A+\bar{A}))+(\bar{\bar{A}}+F) = \text{A}$$

29. $Prove\ the\ following,\ \ ((A\ AND\ A)\ AND\ (B\ OR\ B))\ OR\ (A\ AND\ B) = NOT\ B,$
$where\ A = False\ and\ B\ is\ True$

30. Find C OR (C AND (A AND B)) if A is 00100101, B is 11000101 and C is 01100000.

31. Prove the following (A AND B) AND C if A = 11010101, B is 11001101 and C is 01100100.

32. Find (A OR B) AND (A OR NOT B) where A is FFTFFFT and B is TTFFTFF

33. Find (B OR NOT C) OR (A OR NOT B) AND (C OR NOT A) if A is 110101, B is 100110 and C is 000111.

34. Find (A OR NOT B) OR (C OR NOT NOT A) if A is 100101, B is 100110 and C is 000111.

35. Find (A AND NOT C) OR (C AND NOT C) OR (A AND NOT NOT A) A = TFFFT, C = TFTFF

36. Find (B OR NOT C) OR (A OR NOT B) AND (C OR NOT A) if A is 100110, B is 100110 and C is 000111.

37. Find (A + B) AND NOT (A AND B) if A is TTTFF and B is FFFTT
where T represents True and F represents False

38. *Simplify* $(A+\overline{B})(A+B)+(A\bar{A})+\bar{\bar{A}}$

39. $Prove\ the\ following,\quad ((A\ AND\ B)\ AND\ (A\ AND\ B))\ OR\ (A\ AND\ B) = B,$
$where\ A = True\ and\ B\ is\ False$

40. $Simplify$ $\quad A(\bar{A}B + B) + C\ where\ C = 0$

41. *Simplify* $A(\bar{A} + B) + A\bar{B} = A\bar{A} + AB + A\bar{B}$

42. *Does the following obey associative property* $\overline{(\overline{A + B})} + C$

43. *Find* $((A(B+\bar{B}))(A+\bar{A}))+(\bar{\bar{A}}+F)\bar{A}$

44. *Simplify* $A(\bar{A}+B)+A\bar{B}+\bar{A}=A\bar{A}+AB+A\bar{B}+\bar{A}$

45. *Prove that* $\overline{((A(B+\bar{B}))(A+\bar{A}))}+\bar{B}$

46. Prove that (AB)C =A(BC) prove associative law. Where A = T, B = T, C = F

47. Prove that (A+B) +C = A+(B+C) prove associative law. Where A = F, B = T, C = F

48. *Simplify* $BC + C(A + \bar{B}) + \bar{C}$

49. *Simplify* $BC + C(A + \bar{B})$

50. *Prove that* $\overline{((A(B + \bar{B}))(A + \bar{A}))} + \bar{\bar{\bar{B}}} = \overline{AB}$

MK
MATH
KNOTS
Joy of learning...

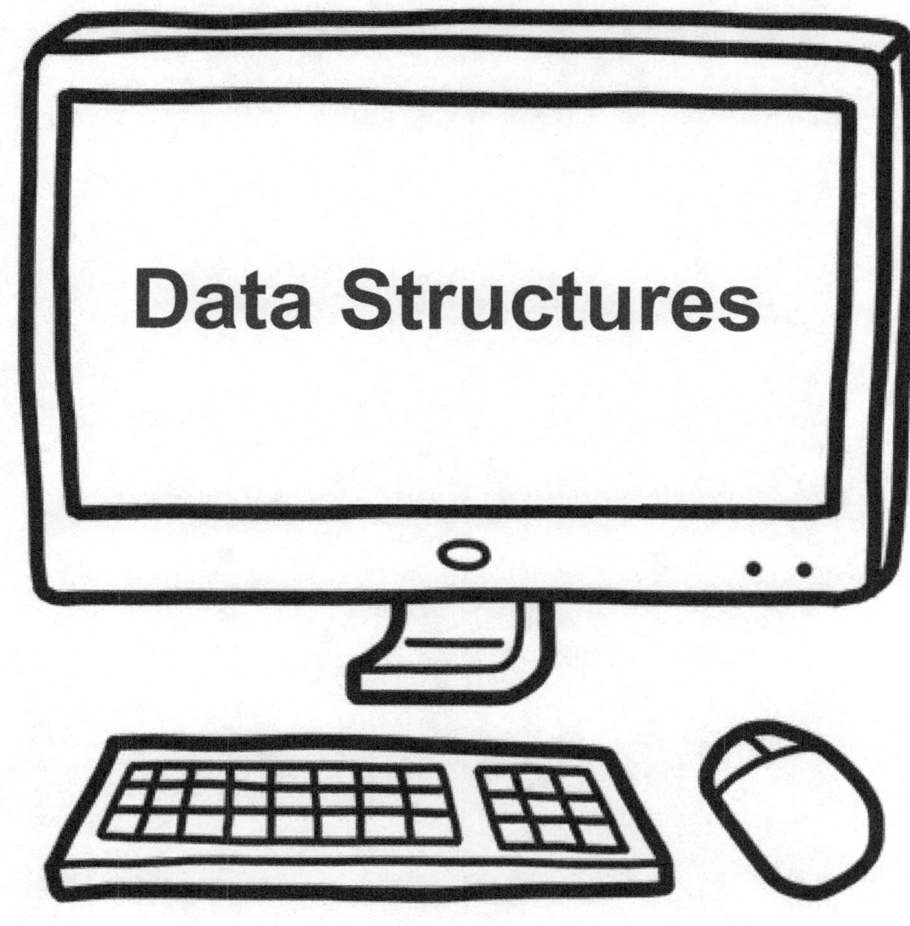
Data Structures

1. What is the value of Z in the following stack?

PUSH(4)

PUSH(5)

PUSH(8)

Y = POP()

X = POP()

PUSH (X-Y)

Z = POP()

2. What is the value of Z in the following stack?

PUSH(2)

PUSH(4)

PUSH(9)

Y = POP()

X = POP()

PUSH (X+Y)

Z = POP()

3. What is the value of Z in the following stack?

PUSH(3)

PUSH(4)

PUSH(7)

Y = POP()

X = POP()

PUSH (X+Y)

Z = POP()

4. What is the value of Z in the following stack?

PUSH(3)

PUSH(4)

PUSH(4)

Y = POP()

X = POP()

Z = POP()

PUSH (X+Y-Z)

M =POP()

5. What is the value of Z in the following stack?

PUSH(9)

PUSH(8)

PUSH(8)

Y = POP()

X = POP()

Z = POP()

PUSH (-X+Y-Z)

M = POP()

6. What is the binary tree for “WEETEDSTER” ?

7. What is the binary tree for “OPINION” ?

8. What is the binary tree for “PROPOSED” ?

9. What is the binary tree for "COPERNICUS" ?

10. What is the binary tree for "TREETRREETT" ?

11. What is the value of Z?

PUSH(4)

PUSH(7)

PUSH(18)

Y = POP()

X = POP()

PUSH (X-Y)

Z = POP()

12. What is the value of Z in the following stack?

PUSH(12)

PUSH(14)

PUSH(19)

Y = POP()

X = POP()

PUSH (X+Y)

Z = POP()

13. What is the value of Z in the following stack?

PUSH(13)

PUSH(24)

PUSH(17)

Y = POP()

X = POP()

PUSH (X+Y)

Z = POP()

14. What is the value of Z in the following stack?

PUSH(13)

PUSH(42)

PUSH(41)

Y = POP()

X = POP()

Z = POP()

PUSH (X+Y - Z)

M = POP()

15. What is the value of Z in the following stack?

PUSH(19)

PUSH(18)

PUSH(8)

Y = POP()

X = POP()

Z = POP()

PUSH (-X+Y-Z)

M = POP()

16. What is the binary tree for " TEERWEERR " ?

17. What is the binary tree for “ LOOPING ” ?

18. What is the binary tree for “ BINARYSEARCH ” ?

19. What is the binary tree for “ 12 23 33 54 43 45 52 ” ?

20. What is the binary tree for “ RETREATRETREAT ” ?

21. Evaluate the following:

Push(5)

Push(9)

Push(pop() + pop())

22. Evaluate the following:

Push(3)

Push(5)

Push(pop() - pop())

23. Evaluate the following:

Push(9)

Push(4)

Push(pop() + pop())

Push(4)

Push (pop() + pop())

24. Evaluate the following:

Push(9)

Push(41)

Push(pop() * pop())

Push(2)

Push (pop() + pop())

25. Evaluate the following:

Push(9)

Push(10)

Push(pop() * pop())

Push(2)

Push (pop() + pop())

26. Aqueue is a ________ (FIFO/LIFO). Fill in the blank.

27. Evaluate the following

Push(2)

Push(9)

Push(pop() * pop())

Push(2)

Push (pop() - pop())

28. Evaluate the following

Push(12)

Push(10)

Push(pop() * pop())

Push(12)

Push (pop() + pop())

Push(10)

Push(pop() +pop())

29. What will be binary tree for: adeffsef ?

30. What will be the binary tree for " 10 12 21 21 12 10 " ?

31. What will be the binary tree for " 123 321 223 332 213 231 " ?

32. What will be the binary tree for " 2229 2992 9922 2299 2292 2229 1112 9992 " ?

33. What will be the binary tree for " 212 112 121 221 210 201 102 120 100 120 " ?

34. What will be the binary tree for " DROPDOWNMENU " ?

35. What will be the binary tree for " CROSSRICHTER " ?

36. What will be the binary tree for " CREEKANDCRACK " ?

37. What will be the binary tree for " 123 321 123 321 123 321 123 321 " ?

38. What will be the binary tree for " 33 23 32 13 31 13 33 11 " ?

39. What will be the binary tree for “ 93 99 100 3999 91 999 31 “ ?

40. What will be the binary tree for “ 144 441 414 441 141 411 414 114 411 “ ?

41. What will be the binary tree for " AFTERMARKETANALYSIS " ?

42. What will be the binary tree for " STACKSANDQUUS " ?

43. What will be the binary tree for " BROOKLYNNEWYORK " ?

44. What will be the binary tree for " COMPUTERALGORITHM " ?

45. Evaluate the following expression:

Push(10)

Push(15)

Push(pop() * pop())

Push(10)

Push (pop() + pop())

Push(15)

Push(pop() +pop())

46. Evaluate the following expression:

Push(121)

Push(101)

Push(pop() + pop())

Push(111)

Push (pop() + pop())

Push(121)

Push(pop() +pop())

47. What will be the binary tree for " ABDOMINOUS " ?

48. What will be the binary tree for " ADMEASUREMENT " ?

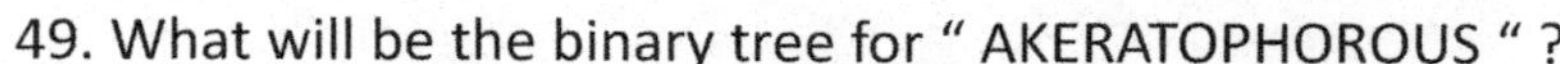

49. What will be the binary tree for " AKERATOPHOROUS " ?

50. What will be the binary tree for " ANAESTHESIOLOGY " ?

MK
MATH
KNOTS
Joy of learning...

What does this program do ?
Arrays

1. What is the output of the below program if the user enters i = 1 2 5 8 ?

```
int Arr[100],n,i,sum=0
        for(i=0;i<n;i++)
        sum+=Arr[i]

Output("\nThe sum of Array is :")<<sum
Output("\nThe average of Array is :")<<sum/i

}
```

2. What is the output of the below program i = 16 10 12 12 14 15 ?

```
{
    int Arr[5],n,i,temp
    temp=Arr[0]
    Arr[0]=Arr[n-1]
    Arr[n-1]=temp
    Output("\nArray after swapping")<<endl
    for(i=0;i<n;i++)
            Output(Arr[i])
}
```

3. What is the output of the below program ?
if the number of elements is 4 and the elements are i = 4 5 8 2 9?

```
{
        Input Arr[100],n,temp,i,j
        for(i=0;j=n-1;i<n/2;i++;j--)
        {
                temp=Arr[i]
                Arr[i]=Arr[j]
                Arr[j]=temp
        }
        Output("\n array")<<endl
        for(i=0 i<n i++)
      Output(Arr[i])


}
```

4. What is the output of the below program
if the elements entered are 5 and the elements are i= 9 8 7 3 5 2 ?

```
        int Arr[100],n,i,small,large
        small=Arr[0]
        large=Arr[0]
        for(i=1;i<n;i++)
        {
                if(Arr[i]<small)
                        small=Arr[i]
                if(Arr[i]>large)
                        large=Arr[i]
        }

        Output("\nelement is :")<<large
        Output("\nelement is :")<<small

}
```

5. What is the output of the program if the elements are 9 10 11 8 10 3 ?

```
{
Int b[5],I,b=0, n=10
Output("Enter the array:")
for(i=0;i<n;i++)
{
Input a[i]
if(a[i]>=10)
b++
}
Output("The number of integers greater or equal to 10 is: ")<<b
}
```

6. What is the output of the below program ?

```
for x = 1:3
 for y = 1:3
    if x==y
      z(x,y) = 1
    elseif x < y
       z(x,y) = 0
    else
       z(x,y) = 1
    end
  end
end
```

7. What is the output of the below program ?

```
for x = 1:3
 for y = 1:3
    if x==y
      z(x,y) = 2
    elseif x < y
       z(x,y) = 0
    else
       z(x,y) = 2
    end
  end
end
```

8. What is the output of the below program ?

```
z = zeros(4)
for x = 1:3
 for y = 1:3
    if x==y
      z(x,y) = x^2 + y^2
    elseif x < y
       z(x,y) = 0
    else
       z(x,y) = x-y
    end
  end
end
```

9. What is the output of the below program ?

```
for x = 1:3
 for y = 1:3
    if x==y
      z(x,y) = x + y
    elseif x < y
       z(x,y) = x
    else
       z(x,y) = y - x
    end
  end
end
```

10. What is the output of the below program ?

```
for x = 1:3
 for y = 1:3
    if x==y
      z(x,y) = y
    elseif x < y
       z(x,y) = y
    else
       z(x,y) = -x
    end
  end
end
```

11. What is the output of the below program ?

```
for x = 1:3
 for y = 1:3
    if x==y
      z(x,y) = y
    elseif x < y
       z(x,y) = y*y
    else
       z(x,y) = x*x
    end
  end
end
```

12. What is the output of the below program ?

```
for x = 1:4
 for y = 1:4
    if x==y
      z(x,y) = x^2 - y^2
    elseif x < y
       z(x,y) = y
    else
       z(x,y) = x
    end
  end
end
```

13. What is the output of the below program ?

```
for x = 1:4
 for y = 1:4
    if x==y
       z(x,y) = x^2
    elseif x < y
       z(x,y) = y
    else
       z(x,y) = y^2
    end
  end
end
```

14. What is the output of the below program ?

```
z = zeros(4)

for x = 1:4
 for y = 1:4
    if x==y
       z(x,y) = y/x
    elseif x < y
       z(x,y) = y
    else
       z(x,y) = x/y
    end
  end
end
```

15. What is the output of the below program ?

```
z = 0.0000

for x = 1:4
 for y = 1:4
    if x==y
      z(x,y) = y/x
    elseif x < y
      z(x,y) = y^2
    else
      z(x,y) = x/y
    end
  end
end
```

16. What is the output of the below program ?

```
for x = 1:4
 for y = 1:4
    if x==y
      z(x,y) = x^2
    else
      z(x,y) = y^x
    end
  end
end
```

17. What is the output of the below program ?

```
for x = 1:4
 for y = 1:4
    if x==y
      z(x,y) = x^2
    else
       z(x,y) = y^x
    end
  end
end
```

18. What is the output of the below program ?

```
for x = 1:4
 for y = 1:4
    if x==y
      z(x,y) = x^2
    else
       z(x,y) = x^2 + y^2

    end
  end
end
```

19. What is the output of the below program ?

```
for x = 1:4
 for y = 1:4
    if x==y
      z(x,y) = x^2
    else
        z(x,y) = 2*y
    end
  end
end
 Output(z)
```

20. What is the output of the below program ?

```
for x = 1:4
 for y = 1:4
    if x==y
      z(x,y) = x^2
    elseif x < y
        z(x,y) = x^2
    else
      z(x,y) = y^2
    end
  end
end
 Output (z)
```

21. What is the output below program ?

```
for x = 1:4
 for y = 1:4
    if x==y
      z(x,y) = x + y
    elseif x < y
       z(x,y) = x^2
    else
      z(x,y) = y + x
    end
 end
end
 Output (z)
```

22. What is the output of the below program ?

```
for x = 1:4
 for y = 1:4
    if x==y
      z(x,y) = x + y
    elseif x < y
       z(x,y) = x*y
    else
      z(x,y) = y + x
    end
 end
end
 Output (z)
```

23. What is the output of the below program ?

```
for x = 1:4
 for y = 1:4
    if x==y
      z(x,y) = x+y
    elseif x < y
        z(x,y) = x*y
    else
       z(x,y) = y*x
    end
 end
end
 Output (z)
```

24. What is the output of the below program ?

```
for x = 1:4
 for y = 1:4
    if x==y
      z(x,y) = x/y
    elseif x < y
        z(x,y) = x*x
    else
       z(x,y) = y*x
    end
 end
end
 Output (z)
```

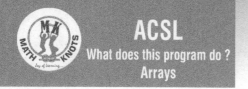

25. What is the output of the below program ?

```
for x = 1:4
 for y = 1:4
    if x==y
      z(x,y) = x*y
    elseif x < y
       z(x,y) = x*x
    else
      z(x,y) = y*y
    end
  end
end
 Output (z)
```

26. What is the output of the below program ?

```
z = 0.0000

for x = 1:4
 for y = 1:4
    if x==y
       z(x,y) = x/y
    elseif x < y
       z(x,y) = x/x
    else
      z(x,y) = y/x
    end
  end
end
 Output (z)
```

27. What is the output of the below program ?

```
A = 100
B = 10
z = 0.0000
for x = 1:3
 for y = 1:3
    if x<y
      z(x,y) = sqrt(A)
    elseif x > y
       z(x,y) = sqrt(B)
    else
       z(x,y) = sqrt(A+B)
    end
  end
end
Output (z)
```

28. What is the output of the below program ?

A = 10
B = 10
z = 0.0000

for x = 1:3
 for y = 1:3
    if x<y
      z(x,y) = $\sqrt{A}$
    elseif x > y
       z(x,y) = $\sqrt{B}$
    else
       z(x,y) = $\sqrt{(\frac{A}{B})}$
    end
  end
end
Output(z)

29. What is the output of the below program ?

```
A = 8
B = 10
z = 0.0000

for x = 1:3
 for y = 1:3
    if x < y
      z(x,y) = sqrt(A*B)
    elseif x > y
       z(x,y) = sqrt(B)
    else
       z(x,y) = sqrt(A/B)
    end
  end
end
Output(z)
```

30. What is the output of the below program ?

```
A = 121
B = 121


for x = 1:5
 for y = 1:5
    if x<y
      z(x,y) = sqrt(A/B)
    elseif x > y
       z(x,y) = sqrt(B/A)
    else
       z(x,y) = sqrt(A/B)
    end
  end
end
Output(z)
```

31. What is the output of the below program ?

```
A = 5
B = 5

for x = 1:3
 for y = 1:3
    if x<y
      z(x,y) = sqrt(A*B)
    elseif x > y
       z(x,y) = sqrt( B/A )
    else
       z(x,y) = B
    end
  end
end
Output(z)
```

32. What is the output of the below program ?

```
A = 9
B = 25

for x = 1:3
 for y = 1:3
    if x<y
      z(x,y) = sqrt(A*B)
    elseif x > y
       z(x,y) = sqrt(B)
    else
       z(x,y) = B
    end
  end
end
Output(z)
```

33. What is the output of the below program 3 5 6 2 4 ?

```
{
        int Arr[100],n,i,s=0
}       for(i=0;i<n;i++)
                sum+=Arr[i]
        Output(s)
}
```

34. What is the output of the below program ?

```
A = 3
B = 5

for x = 1:3
 for y = 1:3
   if x < y
     z(x,y) = sqrt(B)
   elseif x > y
     z(x,y) = A + B
   else
     z(x,y) = B
   end
 end
end
Output(z)
```

35. What is the output of the below program ?

```
A = 3
B = 3

for x = 1:3
 for y = 1:3
    if x < y
      z(x,y) = sqrt(B)
    elseif x > y
      z(x,y) = B^2
    else
      z(x,y) = B
    end
  end
end
Output(z)
```

36. What is the output of the below program ?

```
A = 5
B = 5

for x = 1:3
 for y =1:3
    if x<y
      z(x,y) = B*2
    elseif x > y
      z(x,y) = B^2
    else
      z(x,y) = A^2
    end
  end
end
Output(z)
```

37. What is the output of the below program ?

```
A = 9
B = 14

for x = 1:3
 for y = 1:3
    if x < y
      z(x,y) = B/A
    elseif x > y
       z(x,y) = B-A
    else
       z(x,y) = A+B
    end
  end
end
Output(z)
```

38. What is the output of the below program ?

```
A = 4
B = 4

for x = 1:4
 for y = 1:4
    if x < y
      z(x,y) = A^2
    elseif x > y
       z(x,y) = B^2
    else
       z(x,y) = A + B
    end
  end
end
Output(z)
```

39. What is the output of the below program ?

```
A = 4
B = 4

for x = 1:4
 for y = 1:4
    if x < y
      z(x,y) = A/2
    elseif x > y
       z(x,y) = B*2

    else
       z(x,y) = (A + B)/2
    end
  end
end
Output(z)
```

40. What is the output of the below program ?

```
for x = 1:3
 for y = 1:3
    if x==y
      z(x,y) = 0
    elseif x < y
       z(x,y) = 5
    else
       z(x,y) = 7
    end
  end
end
```

41) In the array X given as below with X(1,1) = 4, what is the output of the below program ?

```
FOR I = 1 TO 4
    FOR J = 1 TO 4
        IF X(I,J)/5 = INT ( X(I,J)/5 )
            THEN X(I,J) = X(I,J)/5
        ELSE X(I,J) = X(I,J) - 1
        IF X(I,J) < 0
            THEN X(I,J) = (ABS(X(I,J)))/5
        ELSE X(I,J) = 2 * X(I,J)
    NEXT J
NEXT I
END
```

-4	20	30	40
20	-9	30	40
20	30	-14	40
20	30	40	-19

42) In the array X given as below with X(1,1) = 2,

what is the output of the below program ?

```
S = 0
FOR I = 1 TO 3
    FOR J = 1 TO 3
        IF X(I,J) = INT (X(I,J))
            THEN X(I,J) = X(I,J)*2
        ELSE X(I,J) = X(I,J) + 2
        IF X(I,J) < 0
            THEN X(I,J) = (ABS(X(I,J))) *2
        ELSE X(I,J) = 2 * X(I,J)
        S = S + X(I,J)
    NEXT J
NEXT I
END
PRINT S
```

2	**-2**	**-4**
-2	**2**	**-2**
-4	**-2**	**2**

43. What is the output of the below program ?

```
for I = 1 to 4
        for J = 1 to 4
                A(I,J) = 2 * I
                B(I,J) = 3 * J
                C(I,J) = A(I,J) + B(J,I)
        next J
next I
end
```

44. What is the output of the below program ?

```
for i = 1 to 3
        for j = 1 to 3
                A(I,J) = i * i + j * j
                B(I,J) = j * j - i * i
                C(I,J) = A(I,J) - B(J,I)
        next J
next I
end
```

45. In the array X given as below with X(1,1) = -5,
what is the output of the below program ?

```
FOR I = 1 TO 3
    FOR J = 1 TO 3
        IF X(I,J)/5 = INT ( X(I,J)/5 )
            THEN X(I,J) = X(I,J)/5
        ELSE X(I,J) = X(I,J) - 5
        IF X(I,J) < 0
            THEN X(I,J) = (ABS(X(I,J)))*(-1)
        ELSE X(I,J) =  5 * X(I,J)
    NEXT J
NEXT I
END
```

-5	**-5**	**-10**
10	**5**	**-5**
5	**10**	**-5**

MATH KNOTS
Joy of Learning....

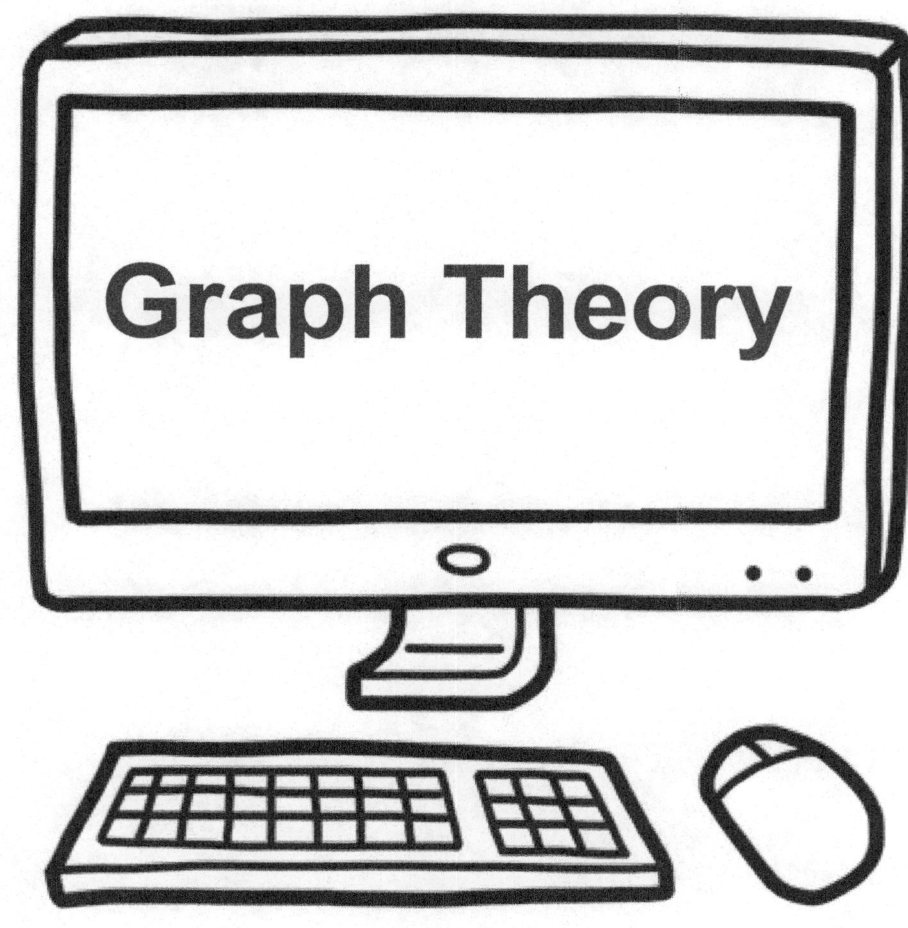
Graph Theory

1. How many paths of length 2 exist in the graph.

2. What are the cyclic closed paths in this graph?

3. What are the closed cyclic paths in this graph?

4. What is the adjacency atrix of the graph?

5. What are the cycles in this graph?

6. How many paths with length 2 exist in the graph?

7. What are the cycles in the graph?

8. What are the cycles in the graph?

9. What are the cycles in the graph?

10. What are the cycles in the graph?

11. What are the cycles in the graph?

12. Draw the graph for the following:

13. What are the cycles in the graph?

14. How many paths of length 2 exist in graph?

15. Is the graph cyclic? Justify?

16. Is there any cycle in this graph?

17. How many paths with length 2 in the graph?

18. Is there a cyclic closed path in this graph?

19. How many paths of length 2 exist in the graph?

20. Is this graph a closed graph?

21. Is the graph a closed graph? Justify

22. What are the cycles in the graph?

23. Does this graph has cyclic closed path?

24. How many paths of length 2 exist in the graph?

25. How many paths of length 2 exist in the graph?

26. What is the adjacency matrix of the graph?

27. Does this graph have a cycle?

28. How many paths of length 2 exist in graph?

29. What are the cycles in the graph?

30. How many paths of length 2 exist in the graph?

31. How many paths of length 2 exist in the graph?

32. What node is directing towards two or more node?

33. How many paths of length 2 exist in graph?

34. Draw the graph:

35. What are the cycles in the graph?

36. What are the cycles in the graph?

37. What are cycles in the graph?

38. Is there a closed cyclic path in the graph?

39. What is the adjacency matrix of the graph?

40. What is the adjacency matrix for the graph?

41. What are the cycles in the graph?

42. What are the cycles in the graph?

43. What is adjacency matrix of the graph?

44. What are the cycles in the graph?

45. What are the cycles in the graph?

46. How many paths of length 2 are in the graph?

47. What are the cycles in the graph?

48. What are the cycles of the graph?

49. What are the cycles in the graph?

50. How many paths of length 2 exist in the graph?

MK
MATH KNOTS
Joy of Learning....

Digital Electronics

1. Simplify the following Logic gate using truth table.

2. Translate into Boolean expression.

3. Simplify the following Logic gate using truth table.

4. Simplify the following Logic gate using the truth table.

5. Translate into Boolean expression.

6. Simplify using truth table.

7. Simplify the Logic gate using truth table.

8. Simplify using truth table.

9. Translate into Boolean expression

10. Translate into Boolean expression.

11. Translate into Boolean expression.

12. Mention the triplets for which the result is TRUE.

13. Translate into Boolean expression.

14. Translate into Boolean expression.

15. Simply using truth table.

16. Translate into Boolean expression.

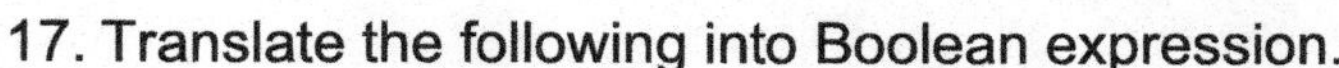

17. Translate the following into Boolean expression.

18. Translate the following Boolean Expression.

19. Find the triplet for which the solution is TRUE

20. Translate the following to Boolean expression.

21. Simplify using truth table.

22. Simplify using truth table.

23. Translate the following to Boolean expression.

24. For which triplets is the solution FALSE

25. Translate into Boolean expression.

26. Simplify using truth table.

27. Translate into Boolean expression.

28. Translate using Boolean expression.

29. Translate into Boolean expression.

30. Simplify using truth table.

31. Translate the following into Boolean.

32. Simplify using truth table. For which triplets is the solution TRUE

33. Translate the expression.

34. Translate into Boolean expression.

35. Simplify the expression using truth table.

36. Translate the following into Boolean expression.

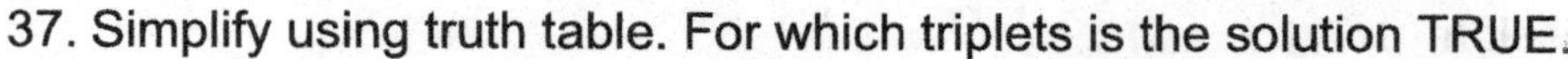

37. Simplify using truth table. For which triplets is the solution TRUE.

38. Translate into Boolean expression.

39. Translate into Boolean expression.

40. Translate the logic gate in Boolean expression.

41. Simplify using truth table.

42. Translate into Boolean expression.

43. Simplify using truth table.

44. Translate into Boolean expression.

45. Simplify using truth table.

46. Translate the following into Boolean expression.

47. Simplify using truth table.

48. Simplify using truth table.

49. Translate the following into Boolean expression.

50. Translate into Boolean expression.

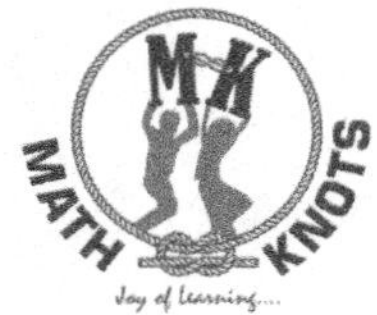
MK
MATH
KNOTS
Joy of Learning....

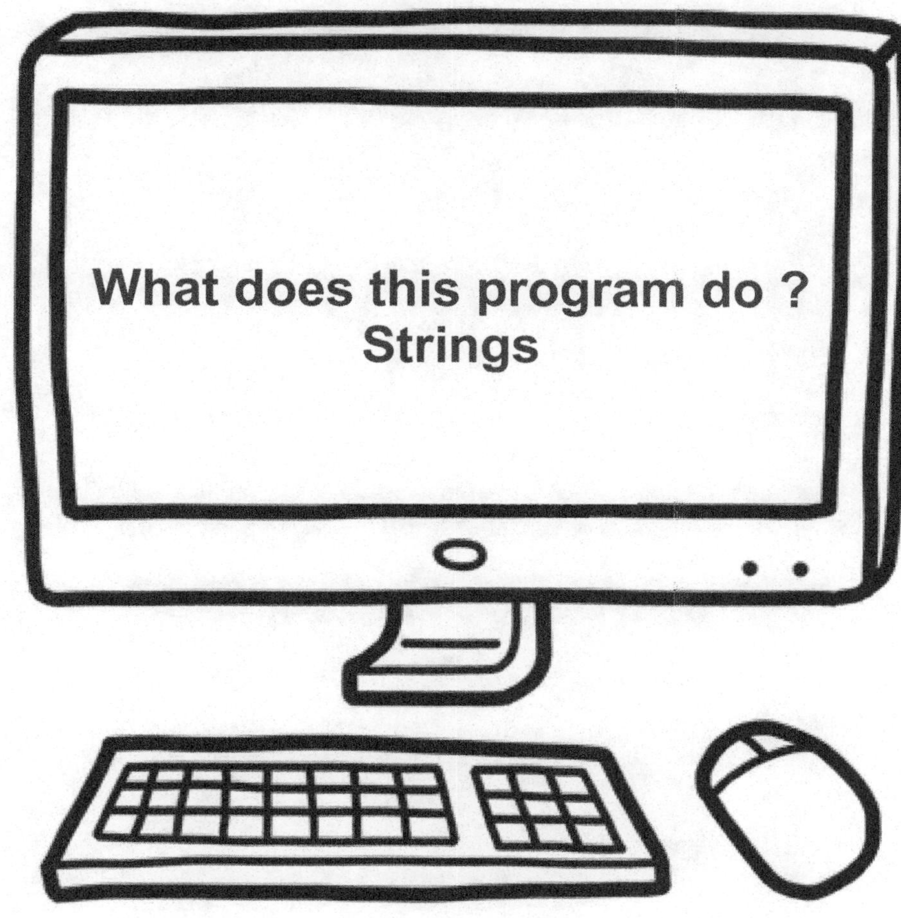
What does this program do ?
Strings

1) What is the output of the below program?

```
B = "BANANASBANANASBANANAS"
T = "" : U = "" : V = "": W = ""
for  I = len(B) – 1 to  0 step -1
 T[I:I] = T[I:I] + B [I:I]
Next I
END
for  I = 0 to len(B) – 1
  IF T[I:I] = "A"
    THEN U = U + T[I:I]
  ELSEIF T[I:I] = "N"
     V[I:I] = V[I:I] + T[I:I]
  ELSE
    W[I:I] = W[I:I] + T[I:I]
  END
next I
PRINT U
PRINT V
PRINT W
END
```

2) What is the output of the below program?

```
B = "LETITSNOWLETITSNOW"
T = "" : U = "" : V = "": W = ""
for I = len(B)  – 1 to  0 step -1
 T[I:I] = T[I:I] + B [I:I]
Next I
END
for I = 0 to len(B)  – 1
  IF T[I:I] = "L" OR T[I:I] = "E" OR T[I:I] = "T"
    THEN U[I:I] = U[I:I] + T[I:I]
  ELSE
     V[I:I] = V[I:I] + T[I:I]
 END
next I
PRINT U
PRINT V
END
```

3) What is the output of the below program?

```
B = "GOGREENSAVEEARTH"
T = "" : U = "" : V = "": W = ""
for I = len(B) – 1 to 0 step -1
 T[I:I] = T[I:I] + B [I:I]
Next I
END
for I = 0 to len(B) – 1
  IF T[I:I] = "A" OR T[I:I] = "E" OR T[I:I] = "O"
    THEN U[I:I] = U[I:I] + T[I:I]
  ELSE
     V[I:I] = V[I:I] + T[I:I]
 END
next I
PRINT U
PRINT LEN[U]
PRINT V
PRINT LEN[V]
END
```

4) What is the output of the below program?

```
B = "YENOMONEY"
T = "" : U = "" : V = "": W = ""
for I = len(B) – 1 to 0 step -1
 T[I:I] = T[I:I] + B [I:I]
Next I
END
for I = 0 to len(B) – 1
  IF T[I:I] = "E" OR T[I:I] = "O"
    THEN U[I:I] = U[I:I] + T[I:I]
  ELSE
     V[I:I] = V[I:I] + T[I:I]
  END
 NEXT I
PRINT U
PRINT LEN[U]
PRINT V
PRINT LEN[V]
END
```

5) What is the output of the below program?

```
char line [100]
int v ,u
i = "enter the string"
for (int i = 0; line[I] !='\0'; ++i)
{
 if (line[i] == 'a' || line[i] == 'e' || line [i] == 'i' || line[i] == 'o' || line[i] == 'u')
++v
else
++u
}
PRINT v
PRINT u
end
```

6) What is the output of the below program?

```
X = ""
Y = ""
string firstname = "Weasley"
string lastname = "Manny"
string fullname = firstname + lastname
fullname += "Jr"
string fullname += '.'
  FOR I= 0 TO LEN [fullname] – 1

        X[I:I]  = X[I:I] + fullname
      NEXT I
   END
   FOR I= 0 TO LEN [X] – 1
         IF (X[I:I] !=  "E") AND (X[I:I] != "A")

         THEN Y[I:I] = X[I:I] + Y[I:I]
         NEXT I
        END
      PRINT Y
END
```

7) What is the output of the below program?

```
X[I:I]  = "REDROOTPUTUPTOORDER"
T = “” : U = "" : V = "": W = ""
for I = len(B)  – 1 to  0 step -1
 T[I:I] = T[I:I] +X [I:I]
Next I
END
for I = 0 to len( T) – 1
  IF T[I:I] = "E" OR T[I:I] = "O" OR T[I:I] = "U"
    THEN U[I:I]  = U[I:I]  + T[I:I]
  ELSE
     V[I:I]  = V[I:I]  + T[I:I]
  END
 next I
  PRINT U
  PRINT LEN[U]
  PRINT V
  PRINT LEN[V]
END
```

8) What is the output of the below program?

```
char line[100]
int v,c,d
i = ”ihave54codesrunning”
for (int i = 0; line[I] !=’\0’; ++i)
{
 if (line[i] == ’a’ || line[i] == ’e’ || line[i] == ’i’ || line[i] == ’o’ || line[i] == ’u’)
++v
elseif (line[i] = ’0’ && line[i] <= ’9’)
++d
else
++c
}
Display v
Display c
Display d
```

9) What is the output of the below program?

```
T = "RACECARRACECAR"
U = "" : V = ""
for I = 0 to len(B) – 1
  IF T[I:I] = "A" OR T[I:I] = "R"
    THEN U[I:I]  = U[I:I]  + T[I:I]
  ELSE
     V[I:I]  = V[I:I]  + T[I:I]
 END
next I
PRINT U
PRINT V
END
```

10) What is the output of the below program?

```
X = ""
Y = ""
string firstname = "JIMMY"
string lastname = "POTTER"
string fullname = firstname + lastname
fullname += "JRJR"
string fullname += '.'
  FOR I= 0 TO LEN [X] – 1
          X [I:I] = X[I:I] +  fullname
          NEXT I
 END
 FOR I= 0 TO LEN [X[I:I]] – 1
          IF (X[I:I] !=  "E") OR (X[I:I] != "I" OR (X[I:I] != "O")
          THEN Y[I:I] = X[I:I] + Y[I:I]
           NEXT I
          END
  PRINT Y[I:I]
  PRINT LEN[Y[I:I]]
END
```

11) What is the output of the below program?

```
X = "ROSSHASGONETOVEGAS"
Y= ""
for I = len(X)  – 1 to  0 step -1
  Y[I:I] = Y + X [I:I]
Next I
PRINT Y
END
```

12) What is the output of the below program?

```
string line
 X[I:I] = "@ASANTA@ 12&%ATNASA@"
 Y[I:I] = "" : Z[I:I] = ""
for I = len(X)  – 1 to  0 step -1
  Y[I:I] = Y[I:I] + X[I:I]
  Next I
End
for I =  0 to len(Y)  – 1  step 1
   IF  Y[I:I] >= A TO Y[I:I] <= Z
    THEN Z[I:I] = Z[I:I] + Y[I:I]
   NEXT
PRINT Z
END
```

13) What is the output of the below program?

```
X[I:I] = "PLASMATELIVISION"
Y = "": Y = "": U = "": T = ""

For I = 0 TO len(X) – 1 step 1
    IF  X[I:I] = "A" OR  X[I:I] = "E" OR  X[I:I] = "I" OR  X[I:I] = "O"
        THEN Z[I:I] = Z[I:I] + Y[I:I]
    ELSEIF
        U[I:I] = U[I:I] + Y[I:I]
    END
NEXT I
  T = U[I:I] + Z[I:I]
        PRINT T
        PRINT LEN[T]
        END
```

14) What is the output of the below program?

```
char line [100]
int v
i = "COMPUTATION"
for (int i = 0; line[I] !='\0'; ++i)
{
 if (line[i] == 'C' || line [i] == 'O' || line[i] == 'T' || line[i] == 'N' || line[i] == 'A')
++v
else
display "Error"
}
Display v
```

15) What is the output of the below program?

```
B = "ANNAANNA"
NUM = 0
T = ""
for I = len(B) – 1 to 0 step -1
T = T + B [I:I]
Next I
end
for I = 0 to len(B) – 1
If A[I:I] == T[I:I] then NUM = NUM + 1
next I
end
print NUM
```

16) What is the output of the below program?

```
string firstname = "Saam"
string lastname = "SeverrusSnnap"
string fullname = firstname + lastname
N = "":
M = ""
A[I:I] = string fullname
FOR i = 0 TO LEN[A]  - 1
      IF A[I:I] != A[I+1: I+1] THEN
         N = N + A[I:I]
      NEXT I
END
FOR I = 0 TO LEN[N]  - 1
   IF N[I:I] > "B"
      THEN M[I:I] = M[I:I] + N[I:I]
   NEXT I
PRINT M
END
```

17) What is the output of the below program?

```
string line
line = "CcOmputer"
for (int i =0; i< line.size(); ++i)
if (!((line[i] >= 'a' && line[i] <= 'z') || (line[i] >= 'A' && line[i] <= 'Z')))
line[i]='\0'
display line
```

18) What is the output of the below program?

```
N = ""
string sentence = "MONTREALINCANADA"
s = sentence.insert(9, " IS ")
FOR I = 0 TO LEN[N] – 1
IF S[I:I] > "E"
   THEN M = M + N[I: I]
   NEXT I
 PRINT LEN[M]
END
```

19) What is the output of the below program?

```
char line[100]
int v,c,d
i = "route 67"
for (int i = 0; line[l] !='\0'; ++i)
{
 if (line[i] == 'a' || line [i] == 'e' || line[i] == 'i' || line[i] == 'o' || line[i] == 'u')
++v
elseif (line[i] >= '0' && line[i] <= '9')
++d
else
++c
}
Display v
Display c
Display d
```

20) What is the output of the below program?

```
str = "SCOOTERPARK"
int c = 0;
For i = 0 to len[str]-1
  c = c + len[str[i:i]]
display c
```

21) What is the output of the below program?

```
string line
line = "l1kel1h00d"
N = ""
for (int i = 0; i < line.size(); ++i)
  for i = 0 to len[line] - 1
    if (!((line[i] >= 'a' && line[i] <= 'z') || (line[i] >= 'A' && line[i] <= 'Z')))
   N = N + line[i,j]
   next
 end
next
PRINT N
PRINT len[N]
end
```

22) What is the output of the below program?

```
char line [100]
N = ''''
line = "notebook"
for (i = 0 to len[line] - 1)
{
 if (line[i,j] == 'a' || line [i,j] == 'e' || line[i,j] == 'i' || line[i,j] == 'o' || line[i,j] == 'u')
 then N = N + line[i,j]
}
next i
  PRINT len[N]
end
```

23) What is the output of the below program?

```
B = "madammillermadam"
NUM = 0
T = ""
S = ""
For i = len(B) – 1 to  0 step -1
 if B[i:i] > "e"
     then T = T + B [i:i]
Next i
For i = 0 to len(T) – 1
If T[i:i] != "m"
     then S = S + T[i:i]
next i
PRINT S
PRINT len[S]
```

24) What is the output of the below program?

```
string line
line = "Aerop12nE"
for (int i =0; i< line.size(); ++i)
   if (!((line[i] >= 'a' && line[i] <= 'z') || (line[i] >= 'A' && line[i] <= 'Z')))
    next
  PRINT line
end
```

25) What is the output of the below program?

```
line = ”p2.’67reep2weep”
for (int i = 0; i < line.size(); ++i)
if (!((line[i] >= ‘a’ && line[i] <= ’z’) || (line[i] >= ‘A’ && line[i] <= ’Z’)))
line[i] =’\0’
display line
```

26) What is the output of the below program?

```
char line[100]
int v,c,d
i = ”34 rue sherbrooke”
for (int i = 0; line[I]!=’\0’; ++i)
{
 if (line[i] == ’a’ || line [i] == ’e’ || line[i] == ’i’ || line[i] == ’o’ || line[i] == ’u’)
++v
elseif (line[i] = ’0’ && line[i] <= ’9’)
++d
else
++c
}
Display v
Display c
Display d
```

27) What is the output of the below program?

```
X = "NOELSEESLEON"
NUM=0
T = ""
S = ""
For i = len(X) – 1 to  0 step -1
  if X[i:i] > "d"
       then T = T + B [i:i]
Next i
For i = 0 to len(T) – 1
    If T[i:i] != "N"
       then S = S + T[i:i]
  next i
PRINT S
PRINT len[S]
end
```

28) What is the output of the below program?

```
char line [100]
V = ""
U = ""
X = "dataanalyticsanalyticsanalyticsdata"
FOR I = 0 TO LEN[X] – 1
IF X[I: I] = "a" or X[I: I] = "e" or X[I: I] = "i" or X[I: I] = "o" or X[I: I] = "u"
  THEN V = V + X[I: I]
ELSE
    U = U + X[I: I]
NEXT I
PRINT "V = " V
PRINT "LV = " LEN[V]
PRINT "U = " U
PRINT "LU = " LEN[U]
```

29) What is the output of the below program?

```
string firstname = "SAAMM"
string middlename = "PPOOEETRRYY"
string lastname = " POOTTERPOETRRY "
string Initial = "MRR."
string fullname = Initial + middlename + firstname + lastname
N= "":
M= ""
A[i,j] = string fullname
FOR i = 0 TO LEN[A]  - 1
                    IF A[I:I] != A[I + 1: I + 1] THEN
N = N + A[I:I]
NEXT I
FOR I = 0 TO LEN[N]  - 1
IF (N[I:I] > "C" THEN M = M + N[I:I]
NEXT I
PRINT fullname
PRINT N
PRINT M
END
```

30) What is the output of the below program?

```
string line
line = "aBSsD./W\POOK"
for (int i = 0; i < line.size(); ++i)
if (!((line[i] >= 'a' && line[i] <= 'z') || (line[i] >= 'A' && line[i] <= 'Z')))
line[i] = '\0'
display line
```

31) What is the output of the below program?

```
B = "CRAZYR00MROOM50921NUMBER770001008"
T = ""
S = ""
U = ""
V = ""
For I = len(B) – 1 to  0 step -1
  if B[I:I] >= "A" || [I:I] >= "0"
       then T = T + B [I:I]
Next I
For i = 0 to len(T) – 1
If T[I:I] = "A" or T[I:I] = "E" or T[I:I] = "I" or T[I:I] = "O" or T[I:I] = "U"
       then S = S + T[I:I]
else if T[I:I] >= 0 and T[I:I] <= 9
       then U =  U + T[I:I]
else
      V = V + T[I:I]
next i
PRINT S
PRINT "LS = " len[S]
PRINT "U = " U
PRINT "LU = " len[U]
PRINT V
PRINT "LV = " len[V]
end
```

32) What is the output of the below program?

```
A = "THEUSAINNORTHAMERICA"
B = "THEAMERICANCONTINENT"
X = ""
Y = ""
FOR I = 0 TO LEN[A] – 1
IF A[I: I] < B[I: I]
  THEN X[I:I] = X[I:I] + A[I:I]
ELSE  X[I:I] = X[I:I] + B[I:I]
NEXT I
FOR I = 0 TO LEN[X] – 1
  IF X[I: I] > "D" THEN Y = Y + X[I: I]
NEXT I
 PRINT " X = " X
 PRINT " Y = " Y
 PRINT "Length (Y) = " LEN[Y]
END
```

33) What is the output of the below program?

```
string line
line = "OOutput OString701"
for (int i = 0; i< line.size(); ++i)
if (!((line[i] >= 'a' && line[i] <= 'z') || (line[i] >= 'A' && line[i] <= 'Z')))
line[i]='\0'
display line
```

34) What is the output of the below program?

```
X = "CCOOOMPUTTTINNGNUUMBERRSS"
Y = ""
Z = ""
FOR I = 0 TO LEN[X] – 1
IF X[I:I] > "E" THEN Y = Y + X[I:I]
   Z = Z + len[Y]
NEXT I
   PRINT "Y = "  Y
   PRINT "Length (Y) = " Z
END
```

35) What is the output of the below program?

```
B = "001DATAMINNINGGINMILLEANNIUM2020"
T = ""
S = ""
U = ""
V = ""
For I = len(B) – 1 to  0 step -1
 if B[I:I] >= "A" || B[I:I] >= "0"
      then T[I:I] = T[I:I] + B[I:I]
Next i
end
For I = len(T) – 1 to 0
    If T[I:I] = "A" or T[I:I] = "E" or T[I:I] = "I" or T[I:I] = "O" or T[I:I] = "U"
      then S = S + T[I:I]
    else if T[I:I] >= 0 and T[I:I] <= 9
      then U =  U + T[I:I]
    else
      V = V + T[I:I]
next i
  PRINT S
  PRINT "LS = " len[S]
 PRINT "U = " U
 PRINT "LU = " len[U]
 PRINT V
 PRINT "LV = " len[V]
end
```

36) What is the output of the below program?

```
X = "22222BLUEBERRYAND33333APPLEBERRIES"
T = ""
S = ""
U = ""
V = ""
For I = len(X) – 1 to  0 step -1
 if X[I:I] >= "A" || X[I:I] >= "0"
      then T[I:I]  = T[I:I] + X[I:I]
Next I
For I = 0 to len(T) – 1
If T[I:I] = "A" or T[I:I] = "E" or T[I:I] = "I" or T[I:I] = "O" or T[I:I] = "U"
      then S = S + T[I:I]
else if T[I:I] >= 0 and T[I:I] <= 9
      then U =  U + T[I:I]
else
     V = V + T[I:I]
next I
PRINT S
PRINT "LS = " len[S]
PRINT "U = " U
PRINT "LU = " len[U]
PRINT V
PRINT "LV = " len[V]
end
```

37) What is the output of the below program?

```
string line
line = "OutpU.tstri7g"
for (int i =0; i< line.size(); ++i)
if (!((line[i] >= 'a' && line[i] <= 'z') || (line[i] >= 'A' && line[i] <= 'Z')))
line[i]='\0'
display line
```

38) What is the output of the below program?

```
char line[100]
int v,c,d
line = "actualement"
for (int i = 0; line[I]! ='\0'; ++i)
{
 if (line[i] == 'a' || line [i] == 'e' || line[i] == 'i' || line[i] == 'o' || line[i] == 'u')
++v
elseif (line[i] = '0' && line[i] <= '9')
++d
else
++c
}
Display v
Display c
Display d
```

39) What is the output of the below program?

```
string line
line = "23He11HeA7en"
for (int i = 0; i < line.size(); ++i)
if (!((line[i] >= 'a' && line[i] <= 'z') || (line[i] >= 'A' && line[i] <= 'Z')))
line[i]='\0'
display line
```

40) What is the output of the below program?

```
A = "KAY AKK AYA KIN  GKAY AKIN "
B = "KIT  EKO TEK  ETO KITE  KOTE"
X = ""
Y = ""
FOR I = 0 TO LEN[A] – 1
IF A[I:I] < B[I:I]
THEN X[I:I] = X[I:I] + A[I:I]
ELSE  X[I:I] = X[I:I] + B[I:I]
NEXT I
FOR I = 0 TO LEN[N] – 1
IF X[I: I] > "D" THEN Y[I:I] = Y[I:I] + X[I: I]
NEXT I
PRINT ' X = '  X
PRINT ' Y = '  Y
PRINT ' Length (Y) = ' LEN[Y]
END
```

41) What is the output of the below program?

```
X = ”STRINGYSTRINGSTRINGYSTRINGE”
Y = ""
Z = “”
For I = 0  to len(X) – 1
  if X[I:I] != "S"
       then Y = Y + X[I:I]
   else
       Z = Z+X[I:I]
Next I
PRINT ' Y = '  Z
PRINT ' Z = '  Z
PRINT 'Length = ' len[Y]
end
```

42) What is the output of the below program if the user entered “Lauren”?

```
X = "NOLEMON,NOMELON,NOLEMON,NOMELON"
T = “”
For I = len(X) – 1 to  0 step -1
 if X[I:I] >= "A" OR X[I:I] = ","
      then T[I:I] = T[I:I] + X[I:I]
Next I
PRINT 'T = ' T
PRINT "LT = " len[T]
end
```

43) What is the output of the below program?

```
X = "NOMISTSORFROSTSIMON"
T = ""
For I = len(X) – 1 to  0 step -1
 if X[I:I] >= "A" OR X[I:I] = ","
       then T[I:I]  = T[I:I] + X [I:I]
 Next I
PRINT 'T = ' T
PRINT "LT = " len[T]
end
```

44) What is the output of the below program?

```
X = "MERRYANDBRIGHTJOYTOTHEWORLD"
T = ""
U = ""
For I = 0 to len(X) – 1 step 1
 if X[I:I] = "A" OR X[I:I] = "E" OR X[I:I] = "O"
       then T[I:I] = T[I:I] + X[I:I]
  else
 U[I:I] = U[I:I] + X[I:I]
Next I
   PRINT 'T = ' T
   PRINT "LT = " len[T]
   PRINT 'U = ' U
   PRINT "LU = " len[U]
end
```

45) What is the output of the below program?

```
X = "NATUREISWRITTENINMATHEMATICALLANGUAGE"
T = ""
U = ""
For I = 0 to len(X) – 1 step 1
   if X[I:I] < S
      then T[I:I] = T[I:I] + X[I:I]
   else
       U[I:I] = U[I:I] + X[I:I]
    Next I
       PRINT 'T = ' T
       PRINT "LT = " len[T]
       PRINT 'U = ' U
       PRINT "LU = " len[U]
   end
end
```

46) What is the output of the below program if the user entered "Noah"?

```
string name = "Neel"
input string uname
while (true)
if uname == name
display "Same name"
else
display "Different name"
```

47) What is the output of the below program?

```
X = "TENDIPARAPIDNET"
Y = “”: Z = “”: T = "" : U = ""
FOR I = 0 TO LEN [X] - 2
                Y[I:I] = X[I:I]+ Y[I:I]
        NEXT I
END
FOR I = 0 TO LEN [Y] - 2 STEP 2
       IF  Y[I:I] <  Y[I + 1:I + 1]
         THEN
            T[I:I] = T[I:I] + Y[I + 1: I + 1]
        ELSE
            U[I:I] = U[I:I] + Y[I:I]
        END IF
       NEXT I
  Z[I:I] = Z[I:I] + T[I:I] + U[I:I]
  PRINT Y
  PRINT Z
END
```

48) What is the output of the below program?

```
X = "JOYTOTHEWORLD"
Y = “”: Z = “”
FOR i = LEN [X] - 2 TO 0
       Y = X[i : i] + Y
    NEXT i
  IF Y != "O" OR Y != "A" OR Y != "E"
       THEN Z = Z + Y
  ENDIF
PRINT Y
PRINT Z
END
```

49) What is the output of the below program? what are the unique letters?

```
X = "SLEDGEISDASHINGTHROUGHTHESNOW"
Y = "": Z = ""
FOR i = 7 TO LEN [X] - 1
                Y = X[i:i] + Y
        NEXT i
  IF Y != "O" OR Y != "A" OR Y != "H" OR Y!= "D"
       THEN Z = Z + Y
  ENDIF
PRINT Y
PRINT Z
END
```

50) What is the output of the below program?

```
S = "ROTATORROTATORROTATORS"
Z = 0
X = "": Y = ""
For I = len(B) – 1 to  0 step -1
    X[I:I] = X[I:I] + S[I:I]
Next I
For I = 1 to len(B) – 1
  If S[I:I] == X[I:I]
    Y[I:I] = Y[I:I] + X[I:I]
   then Z[I:I] = Z[I:I] + Len[Y]
 next I
  PRINT " X = "  X
  PRINT " Y = "  Y
  PRINT "Length = " len[Y]
```

MK
MATH
KNOTS
Joy of Learning...

Answer Keys

1. Simplify $C + \overline{BC}$

Solution :

$$C + (\bar{B} + \bar{C}) = (C + \bar{C}) + \bar{B} = T + \bar{B} = T$$

2. *Simplify* $\overline{AC}(\bar{A} + C)(\bar{C} + C)$

Solution :

$$= \overline{AC}(\bar{A} + C)(\bar{C} + C)$$
$$= \overline{AC}(\bar{A} + C) = (\bar{A} + \bar{C})(\bar{A} + C)$$
$$= \bar{A}\bar{A} + \bar{A}C + \bar{C}\bar{A} + \bar{C}C$$
$$= \bar{A} + \bar{A}C + \bar{C}\bar{A} + T = T$$

3. *Simplify* $(A + B)(AD + A\bar{D}) + B$

Solution :

$$= (A + B)A(D + \bar{D}) + B$$
$$= (A + B)A + B$$
$$= A + AB + B$$
$$= A + B(A + T) = A + B$$

4. Find A OR (A AND B) where A is 011101 and B is 101000.

Solution :

A	B	A AND B	A OR (A AND B)
0	1	0	0
1	0	0	1
1	1	1	1
1	0	0	1
0	0	0	0
1	0	0	1

5. Find B AND (A OR (A AND B)) where A is 0101000 and B is 1110101.

Solution :

A	B	A AND B	A OR (A AND B)	B AND (A OR (A AND B))
0	1	0	0	0
1	1	1	1	1
0	1	0	0	0
1	0	0	1	0
0	1	0	0	0
0	0	0	0	0
0	1	0	0	0

6. Find (A OR B) OR (A AND B) where A is 0111100 and B is 1110101.

Solution :

A	B	A OR B	A AND B	(A OR B) OR (A AND B)
0	1	1	0	1
1	1	1	1	1
1	1	1	1	1
1	0	1	0	1
1	1	1	1	1
0	0	0	0	0
0	1	1	0	1

7. Prove the commutative law if A is 0101000 and B is 1110001.

Solution :

A	B	A OR B
0	1	1
1	1	1
0	1	1
1	0	1
0	0	0
0	0	0
0	1	1

B	A	B OR A
1	0	1
1	1	1
1	0	1
0	1	1
0	0	0
0	0	0
1	0	1

It can be observed that A OR B = B OR A. Hence Proved.

8. Find A AND (A OR (A OR B)) if A is 0101000 and B is 1110001.

Solution :

A	B	A OR B	A OR (A OR B)	A AND (A OR (A OR B))
0	1	1	1	0
1	1	1	1	1
0	1	1	1	0
1	0	1	1	1
0	0	0	0	0
0	0	0	0	0
0	1	1	1	0

9 Find C OR (C AND (A AND B)) if A is 01100111 B is 11001101 and C is 01100100

Solution :

A	B	C	A AND B	C AND (A AND B)	C OR (C AND (A AND B))
0	1	0	0	0	0
1	1	1	1	1	1
1	0	1	0	0	1
0	0	0	0	0	0
0	1	0	0	0	0
1	1	1	1	1	1
1	0	0	0	0	0
1	1	0	1	0	0

10. Find A OR (A AND (A AND B)) if A is 01100111 and B is 11001101.

Solution :

A	B	A AND B	A AND (A AND B)	A OR (A AND (A AND B))
0	1	0	0	0
1	1	1	1	1
1	0	0	0	1
0	0	0	0	0
0	1	0	0	0
1	1	1	1	1
1	0	0	0	1
1	1	1	1	1

11. Prove the associative law if A = 10000111, B is 11001101 and C is 01100100.

Solution :

A	B	C	A AND B	(A AND B) AND C
0	1	0	0	0
1	1	1	1	1
0	0	1	0	0
0	0	0	0	0
0	1	0	0	0
1	1	1	1	1
1	0	0	0	0
1	1	0	1	0

A	B	C	B AND C	A AND (B AND C)
0	1	0	0	0
1	1	1	1	1
0	0	1	0	0
0	0	0	0	0
0	1	0	0	0
1	1	1	1	1
1	0	0	0	0
1	1	0	0	0

12. $Simplify$

$$(A + (B + \bar{B}\ ) + \bar{A}\ ) + \bar{\bar{A}}$$

Solution :

$$= (A + (T) + \bar{A}\ ) + \bar{\bar{A}} = (A + \bar{A}\ ) + T + \bar{\bar{A}}$$
$$= T + T + A = T$$

13. $Simplify$

$$((A(B + \overline{B}\ ))(A + \bar{A}\ )) + \bar{\bar{A}}$$

Solution :

$$= ((A(T))(A + \bar{A}\ )) + \bar{\bar{A}}$$
$$= (A)(A + \bar{A}\ )) + \bar{\bar{A}} = (A(T)) + \bar{\bar{A}} = (A(T)) + \bar{\bar{A}} = A + A = \mathrm{A}$$

14. $Prove\ that \quad (AA + \bar{A}\ )\bar{A}\ + \overline{B}\ = \overline{AB}$

Solution :

$$Simplify\ \ L.H.S = (AA + \bar{A}\ )\bar{A}\ + \overline{B}\ =\ (A + \bar{A}\ )\bar{A}\ + \overline{B}$$
$$=\ (T)\bar{A}\ + \overline{B}\ =\ \bar{A}\ + \overline{B}\ = \overline{AB}\ = RHS$$

15. $Simplify \quad (A + A)\bar{A}\ + (\bar{A}\ + A)A$

Solution :

$$= (A)\bar{A}\ + (T)A = F + A = A$$

16. $Simplify \quad ((A(B + NOT\ B))(A + NOT\ A))$

Solution :

$$= ((A(T))(T)) = AT = A$$

17. $Prove\ the\ following{:}\ (NOT\ A + (A + F)) = B + \overline{B}$

Solution :

$$Simplify\ \ L.H.S = (NOT\ A + (A + F)) = (NOT\ A + A) = T$$
$$RHS =\ B + \overline{B}\ = T$$
$$LHS = RHS$$

18. $Simplify \quad (A + \overline{B}\ )(A + B) + (A\bar{A})$

Solution :

$$= AA + AB + \overline{B}\ A + \overline{B}\ B + (A\bar{A}) = A + F + F = \mathrm{A}$$

19. $Prove\ the\ following, ((A\ OR\ B)\ OR\ (A\ AND\ B))AND\ (A\ AND\ B) = B, where\ A = True\ and\ B\ is\ False$

Solution : Substitute $True = 1\ and\ False = 0$

$$((A\ OR\ B)\ OR\ (A\ AND\ B))AND\ (A\ AND\ B) = ((1\ OR\ 0)\ OR\ (1\ AND\ 0))AND\ (1\ AND\ 0)$$
$$= ((1)\ OR\ (0))AND\ (0)$$
$$= (1)AND\ (0) = 0 = B$$

20. $Prove\ the\ following, ((A\ OR\ A)\ AND\ (B\ AND\ B))\ OR\ (A\ AND\ B) = NOT \quad , where\ A = False\ and\ B\ is\ True$

Solution : Substitute $True = 1\ and\ False = 0$

$$((A\ OR\ A)\ AND\ (B\ AND\ B))\ OR\ (A\ AND\ B) = ((0\ OR\ 0)\ AND\ (1\ AND\ 1))\ OR\ (0\ AND\ 1)$$
$$= ((0)\ AND\ (1))\ OR\ (0) = 0 = NOT\ B$$

21. Find A OR NOT (A AND B) if A is TTTFF and B is FFFTT
where T represents True and F represents False

Solution :

A	B	A AND B	NOT (A AND B)	A OR NOT (A AND B)
T	F	F	T	T
T	F	F	T	T
T	F	F	T	T
F	T	F	T	T
F	T	F	T	T

22. Find (A OR B) AND (A OR NOT B)
where A is TFTFFFT and B is FTFFTFF

Solution :

A	B	A OR B	A OR NOT B	(A OR B) AND (A OR NOT B)
T	F	T	T	T
F	T	T	F	F
T	F	T	T	T
F	F	F	T	F
F	T	T	F	F
F	F	F	T	F
T	F	T	T	T

23. Find (B OR NOT C) AND (A OR NOT B) AND (C OR NOT A) if A is 110101, B is 100110 and C is 000111.

Solution :

A	B	C	B OR NOT C	A OR NOT B	C OR NOT A	(B OR NOT C) AND (A OR NOT B) AND (C OR NOT A)
1	1	0	1	1	0	0
1	0	0	1	1	0	0
0	0	0	1	1	1	1
1	1	1	1	1	1	1
0	1	1	1	0	1	0
1	0	1	0	1	0	0

24. Find (A OR NOT B) OR (C OR NOT NOT A) if A is 100101, B is 100110 and C is 000111.

Solution :

A	B	C	A OR NOT B	C OR NOT NOT A	(A OR NOT B) OR (C OR NOT NOT A)
1	1	0	1	1	1
0	0	0	1	0	1
0	0	0	1	0	1
1	1	1	1	1	1
0	1	1	0	1	1
1	0	1	1	1	1

25. Find (A OR NOT NOT B) OR (C OR NOT NOT A) AND (A AND B) if A is 000101, B is 100100, C is 100101.

Solution :

A	B	C	A OR NOT NOT B	C OR NOT NOT A	A AND B	(A OR NOT NOT B) OR (C OR NOT NOT A) AND (A AND B)
0	1	1	1	1	0	0
0	0	0	0	0	0	0
0	0	0	0	0	0	0
1	1	1	1	1	1	1
0	0	0	0	0	0	0
1	0	1	1	1	0	0

26. Find (A OR C) OR (C AND A) AND (A AND B) if A is TTFFT, B is FFTTT and C is TTTTF

Solution :

A	B	C	A OR C	C AND A	A AND B	(A OR C) OR (C AND A) AND (A AND B)
T	F	T	T	T	F	F
T	F	T	T	T	F	F
F	T	T	T	F	F	F
F	T	T	T	F	F	F
T	T	F	T	F	T	T

27. Find (A AND C) OR (C AND NOT C) AND (A AND NOT NOT A) A= TFFFT, C= TFTFF

Solution :

A	C	A AND C	C AND NOT C	A OR NOT NOT A	(A AND C) OR (C AND NOT C) AND (A AND NOT NOT A)
T	T	T	F	T	T
F	F	F	F	F	F
F	T	F	F	F	F
F	F	F	F	F	F
T	F	F	F	T	F

28. *Prove that*

$$((A(B+\bar{B}))(A+\bar{A}))+(\bar{\bar{A}}+F) = A$$

Solution : $((A(B+\bar{B}))(A+\bar{A}))+(\bar{\bar{A}}+F) = ((A(T))(A+\bar{A}))+(\bar{\bar{A}}+F)$

$=(A)(A+\bar{A}))+(\bar{\bar{A}}+F) = (A(T))+(\bar{\bar{A}}+F)$

$= (A(T))+(\bar{\bar{A}}+F) = A+A = A$

29. *Prove the following,* $((A\ AND\ A)\ AND\ (B\ OR\ B))\ OR\ (A\ AND\ B) = NOT\ B,$

$where\ A = False\ and\ B\ is\ True$

Solution : Substitute $True = 1\ and\ False = 0, therefore$

$((A\ AND\ A)\ AND\ (B\ OR\ B))\ OR\ (A\ AND\ B) = ((0\ AND\ 0)\ AND\ (1\ OR\ 1))\ OR\ (0\ AND\ 1)$

$= ((0)\ AND\ (1))\ OR\ (0) = 0 = NOT\ B$

30. Find C OR (C AND (A AND B)) if A is 00100101, B is 11000101 and C is 01100000.

Solution :

A	B	C	A AND B	C AND (A AND B)	C OR (C AND (A AND B))
0	1	0	0	0	0
0	1	1	0	0	1
1	0	1	0	0	1
0	0	0	0	0	0
0	0	0	0	0	0
1	1	0	1	0	0
0	0	0	0	0	0
1	1	0	1	0	0

31. Prove the following (A AND B) AND C if A = 11010101, B is 11001101 and C is 01100100.

Solution :

A	B	C	A AND B	(A AND B) AND C
1	1	0	1	0
1	1	1	1	1
0	0	1	0	0
1	0	0	0	0
0	1	0	0	0
1	1	1	1	1
0	0	0	0	0
1	1	0	1	0

32. Find (A OR B) AND (A OR NOT B) where A is FFTFFFT and B is TTFFTFF

Solution :

A	B	A OR B	A OR NOT B	(A OR B) AND (A OR NOT B)
F	T	T	F	F
F	T	T	F	F
T	F	T	T	T
F	F	F	T	F
F	T	T	F	F
F	F	F	T	F
T	F	T	T	T

33. Find (B OR NOT C) OR (A OR NOT B) AND (C OR NOT A) if A is 110101, B is 100110 and C is 000111.

Solution :

A	B	C	B OR NOT C	A OR NOT B	C OR NOT A	(B OR NOT C) OR (A OR NOT B) AND (C OR NOT A)
1	1	0	1	1	0	0
0	1	1	1	0	1	0
0	0	0	1	1	1	1
1	1	1	1	1	1	1
0	1	1	1	0	1	1
1	0	1	0	1	1	1

34. Find (A OR NOT B) OR (C OR NOT NOT A) if A is 100101, B is 100110 and C is 000111.

Solution :

A	B	C	A OR NOT B	C OR NOT NOT A	(A OR NOT B) AND (C OR NOT NOT A)
1	1	0	1	1	1
0	0	0	1	0	0
0	0	0	1	0	0
1	1	1	1	1	1
0	1	1	0	1	0
1	0	1	1	1	1

35. Find (A AND NOT C) OR (C AND NOT C) OR (A AND NOT NOT A) A = TFFFT, C = TFTFF

Solution :

A	C	A AND NOT C	C AND NOT C	A OR NOT NOT A	(A AND C) OR (C AND NOT C) OR (A AND NOT NOT A)
T	T	F	F	T	T
F	F	F	F	F	F
F	T	F	F	F	F
F	F	F	F	F	F
T	F	T	F	T	T

36. Find (B OR NOT C) OR (A OR NOT B) AND (C OR NOT A) if A is 100110, B is 100110 and C is 000111.

Solution :

A	B	C	B OR NOT C	A OR NOT B	C OR NOT A	(B OR NOT C) OR (A OR NOT B) AND (C OR NOT A)
1	1	0	1	1	0	0
0	0	0	1	1	1	1
0	0	0	1	1	1	1
1	1	1	1	1	1	1
1	1	1	1	1	1	1
0	0	1	0	1	1	1

37. Find (A + B) AND NOT (A AND B) if A is TTTFF and B is FFFTT
where T represents True and F represents False

Solution :

A	B	A AND B	NOT (A AND B)	(A + B) AND NOT (A AND B)
T	F	F	T	T
T	F	F	T	T
T	F	F	T	T
F	T	F	T	T
F	T	F	T	T

38. *Simplify* $(A+\bar{B})(A+B)+(A\bar{A})+\bar{\bar{A}}$

Solution : $= AA + AB + \bar{B}A + \bar{B}B + (A\bar{A}) + \bar{\bar{A}}$
$= A + F + F + A = A + F = A$

39. *Prove the following,* $((A\ AND\ B)\ AND\ (A\ AND\ B))\ OR\ (A\ AND\ B) = B,$
where $A = True$ *and* B *is* $False$

Solution : Substitute $True = 1$ *and* $False = 0$

$$((A\ AND\ B)\ AND\ (A\ AND\ B))\ OR\ (A\ AND\ B) = ((1\ AND\ 0)\ AND\ (1\ AND\ 0))\ OR\ (1\ AND\ 0)$$
$$= ((0)\ OR\ (0))AND\ (0)$$
$$= (0)\ AND\ (0) = 0 = B$$

40. *Simplify* $A(\bar{A}B+B)+C$ *where* $C=0$

Solution : $A(\bar{A}B+B)+C = A\bar{A}B + AB + C = 0 + AB + (0) = AB$

41. *Simplify* $A(\bar{A}+B)+A\bar{B} = A\bar{A} + AB + A\bar{B}$

Solution : $= 0 + A(B+\bar{B}) = A$

42. *Does the following obey associative property* $(\overline{\overline{A+B}})+C$

Solution : $(\overline{\overline{A+B}})+C = (A+B)+C$ *which can be written as* $A+(B+C)$

43. *Find* $((A(B+\bar{B}))(A+\bar{A}))+(\bar{\bar{A}}+F)\bar{A}$

Solution :

$$= ((A(T))(A+\bar{A}))+(\bar{\bar{A}}+F)\bar{A}$$
$$= (A)(A+\bar{A}))+(\bar{\bar{A}}+F)\bar{A} = (A(T))+(\bar{\bar{A}}+F)\bar{A}$$
$$= (A(T))+(\bar{\bar{A}}+F)\bar{A} = A + A\bar{A} = A + F = A$$

44. *Simplify* $A(\bar{A}+B)+A\bar{B}+\bar{A} = A\bar{A}+AB+A\bar{B}+\bar{A}$

Solution : $= 0 + A(B+\bar{B})+\bar{A} = A+\bar{A} = 1$

45. *Prove that* $\overline{((A(B+\bar{B}))(A+\bar{A}))}+\bar{B}$

Solution :

$$= \overline{((A(T))(A+\bar{A}))}+\bar{B} = \overline{(A)(A+\bar{A}))}+\bar{B}$$
$$= \overline{(A(T))}+\bar{B} = \overline{(A(T))}+\bar{B} = \bar{A}+\bar{B} = \overline{AB}$$

46. Prove that (AB)C =A(BC) prove associative law. Where A = T, B = T, C = F
Solution :
(AB)C = (T AND T) AND F = T AND F = F
A(BC) =T AND (T AND F) = T AND F = F
Hence Proved

47. Prove that (A+B) +C = A+(B+C) prove associative law. Where A = F, B = T, C = F
Solution :
(A+B) +C = (F + T) + F = T + F = T
A+(B+C) = F + (T + F) = F + T = T
Hence Proved

48. $Simplify$ $BC + C(A + \bar{B}) + \bar{C}$
Solution :
$$= BC + CA + C\bar{B} + \bar{C} = C(A + B + \bar{B}) + \bar{C}$$
$$= C(A + 1) + \bar{C} = C + \bar{C} = T$$

49. $Simplify$ $BC + C(A + \bar{B})$
Solution :
$$= BC + CA + C\bar{B}$$
$$= C(A + B + \bar{B}) = C(A + 1) = C$$

50. $Prove\ that$ $\overline{((A(B + \bar{B}))(A + \bar{A}))} + \bar{\bar{\bar{B}}} = \overline{AB}$

Solution :
$$= \overline{((A(T))(A + \bar{A}))} + \bar{B}$$
$$= \overline{(A)(A + \bar{A}))} + \bar{B} = \overline{(A(T))} + \bar{B}$$
$$= \overline{(A(T))} + \bar{B} = \bar{A} + \bar{B} = \overline{AB}$$

1. What is the value of Z in the following stack?

PUSH(4)

PUSH(5)

PUSH(8)

Y = POP()

X = POP()

PUSH (X-Y)

Z = POP()

Y = 8

X = 5

PUSH WILL ACT ON X-Y = -3

THE LAST POP REMOVES THE -3 AND STORES IN Z

2. What is the value of Z in the following stack?

PUSH(2)

PUSH(4)

PUSH(9)

Y = POP()

X = POP()

PUSH (X+Y)

Z = POP()

ANSWER:

Y = 9

X = 4

PUSH WILL ACT ON X+Y = 13

THE LAST POP REMOVES THE 13 AND STORES IN Z

3. What is the value of Z in the following stack?

PUSH(3)

PUSH(4)

PUSH(7)

Y = POP()

X = POP()

PUSH (X+Y)

Z = POP()

ANSWER:

Y = 7

X = 4

PUSH WILL ACT ON X+Y = 11

THE LAST POP REMOVES THE 11 AND STORES IN Z

4. What is the value of Z in the following stack?

PUSH(3)

PUSH(4)

PUSH(4)

Y = POP()

X = POP()

Z = POP()

PUSH (X+Y-Z)

M =POP()

ANSWER:

Y = 4

X = 4

Z = 3

PUSH WILL ACT ON X+Y- Z = 5

THE LAST POP REMOVES THE 5 AND STORES IN M

5. What is the value of Z in the following stack?

PUSH(9)

PUSH(8)

PUSH(8)

Y = POP()

X = POP()

Z = POP()

PUSH (-X+Y-Z)

M = POP()

ANSWER:

Y = 8

X = 8

Z = 9

PUSH WILL ACT ON -X+Y-Z = -9

THE LAST POP REMOVES THE -9 AND STORES IN M

6. What is the binary tree for "WEETEDSTER" ?

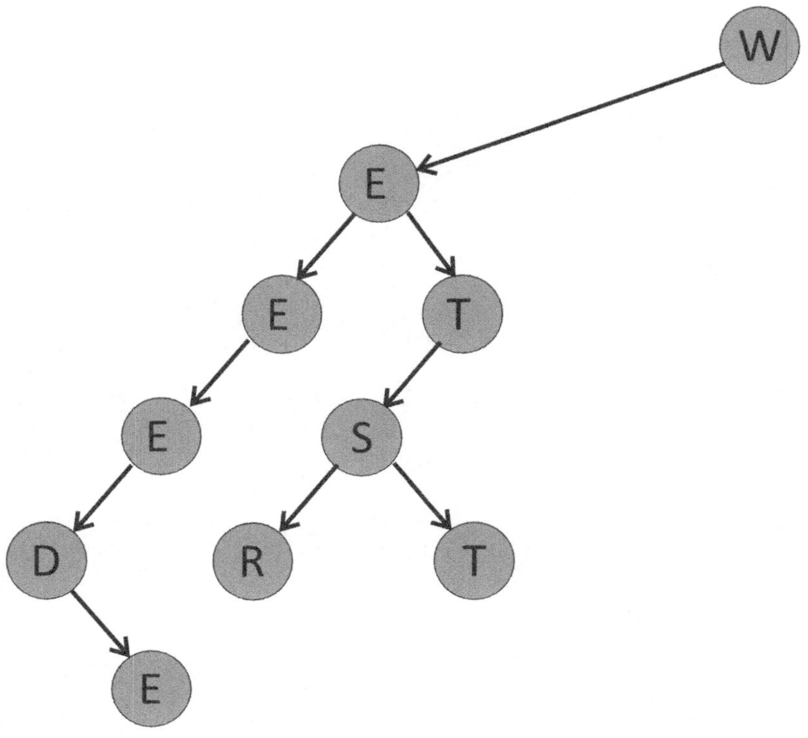

7. What is the binary tree for "OPINION" ?

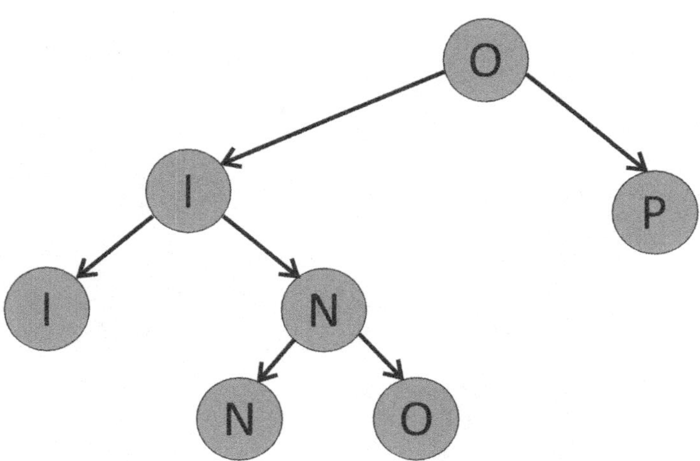

8. What is the binary tree for "PROPOSED" ?

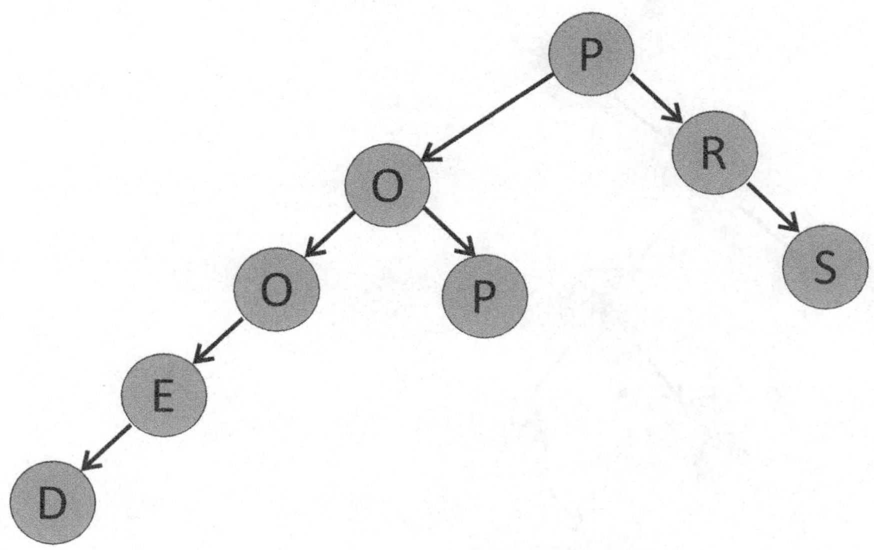

9. What is the binary tree for "COPERNICUS" ?

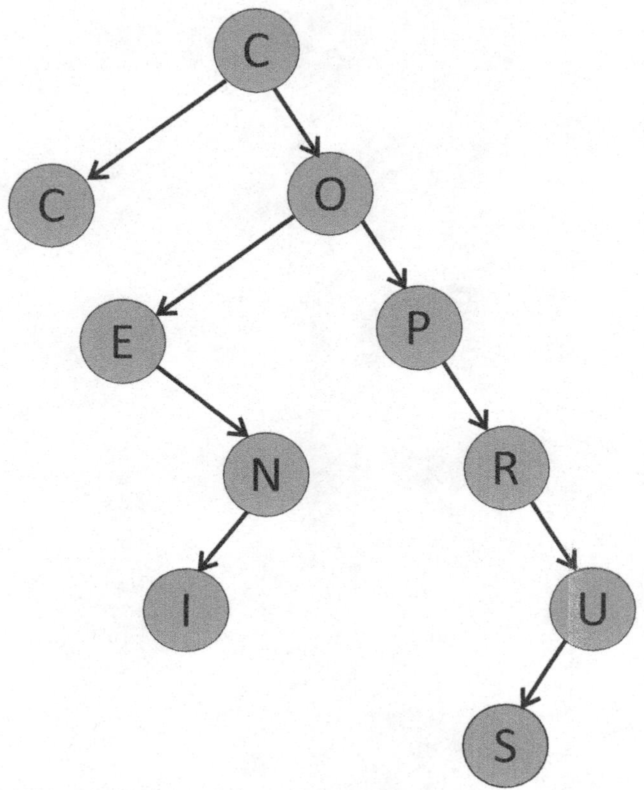

10. What is the binary tree for “TREETRREETT” ?

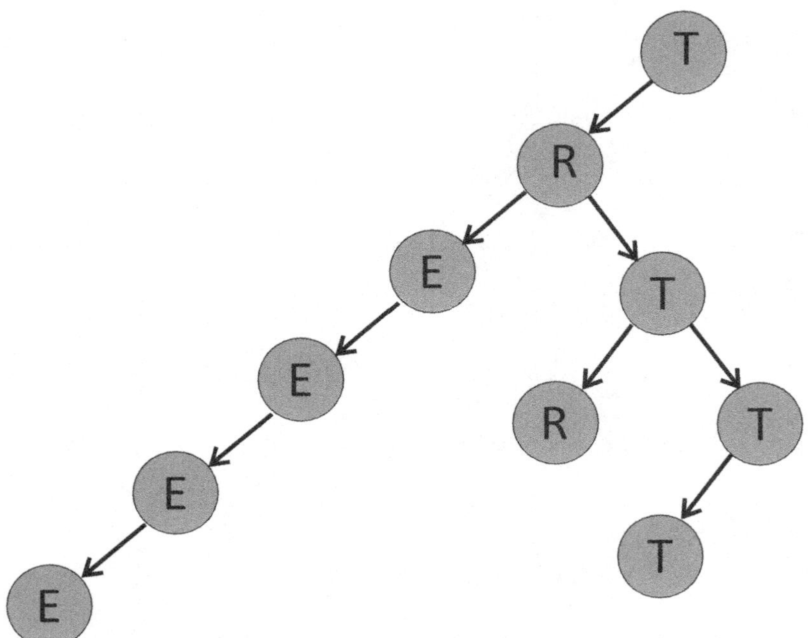

11. What is the value of Z?

PUSH(4)

PUSH(7)

PUSH(18)

Y = POP()

X = POP()

PUSH (X-Y)

Z = POP()

ANSWER:

Y = 18

X = 7

PUSH WILL ACT ON X-Y = -11

THE LAST POP REMOVES THE -11 AND STORES IN Z

12. What is the value of Z in the following stack?

PUSH(12)

PUSH(14)

PUSH(19)

Y = POP()

X = POP()

PUSH (X+Y)

Z = POP()

ANSWER:

Y = 19

X = 14

PUSH WILL ACT ON X+Y = 33

THE LAST POP REMOVES THE 33 AND STORES IN Z

13. What is the value of Z in the following stack?

PUSH(13)

PUSH(24)

PUSH(17)

Y = POP()

X = POP()

PUSH (X+Y)

Z = POP()

ANSWER:

Y = 17

X = 24

PUSH WILL ACT ON X+Y = 41
THE LAST POP REMOVES THE 41 AND STORES IN Z

14. What is the value of Z in the following stack?

PUSH(13)

PUSH(42)

PUSH(41)

Y = POP()

X = POP()

Z = POP()

PUSH (X+Y - Z)

M = POP()

ANSWER:

Y = 41

X = 42

Z = 13

PUSH WILL ACT ON X+Y-Z =70

THE LAST POP REMOVES THE 70 AND STORES IN M

15. What is the value of Z in the following stack?

PUSH(19)

PUSH(18)

PUSH(8)

Y = POP()

X = POP()

Z = POP()

PUSH (-X+Y-Z)

M = POP()

Solution :

Y = 8

X = 18

Z = 19

PUSH WILL ACT ON -X+Y -Z = 9

THE LAST POP REMOVES THE 9 AND STORES IN M

16. What is the binary tree for " TEERWEERR " ?

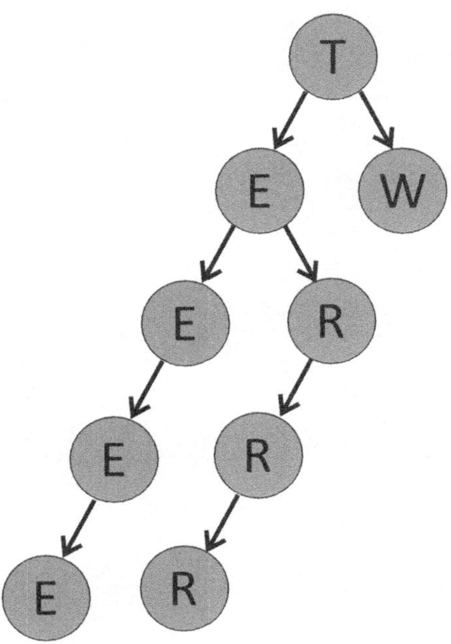

17. What is the binary tree for " LOOPING " ?

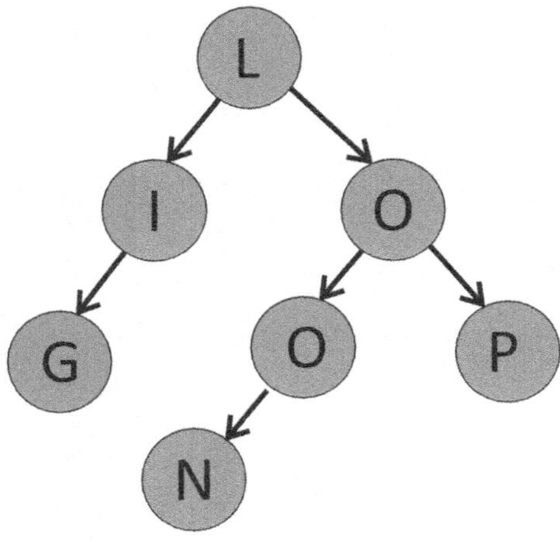

18. What is the binary tree for " BINARYSEARCH " ?

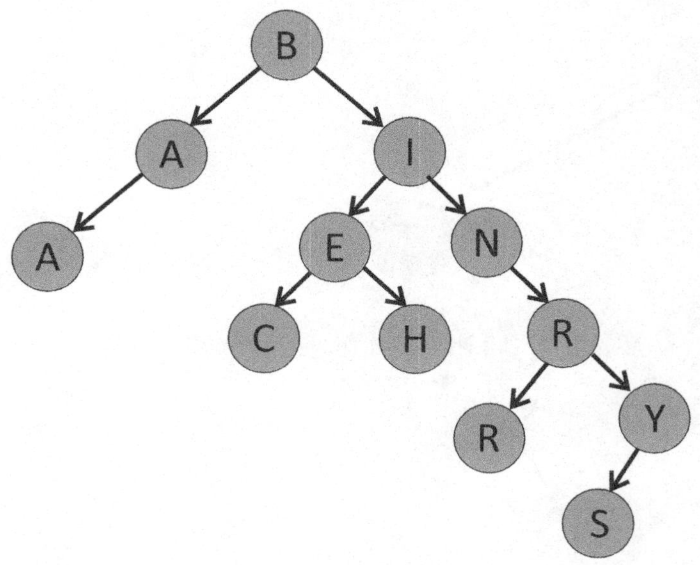

19. What is the binary tree for " 12 23 33 54 43 45 52 " ?

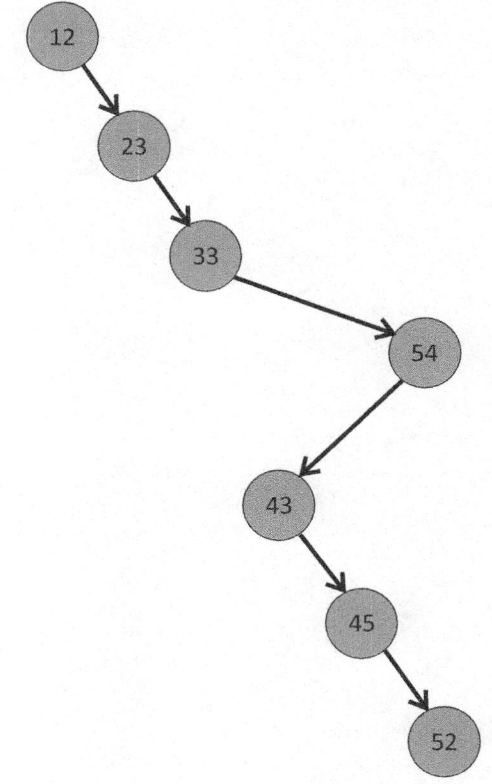

20. What is the binary tree for “ RETREATRETREAT ” ?

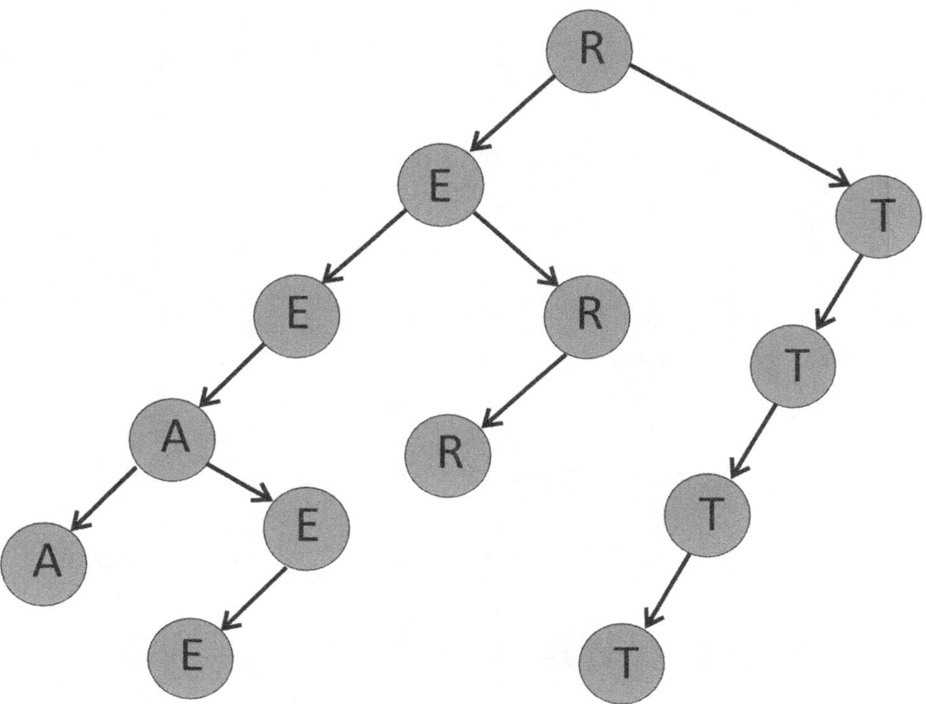

21. Evaluate the following:

Push(5)

Push(9)

Push(pop() + pop())

Answer:

Push(5)	5
Push(9)	9
Push(pop() + pop())	**14**

22. Evaluate the following:

Push(3)

Push(5)

Push(pop() - pop())

Solution :

Push(3)	3
Push(5)	5
Push(pop() – pop())	**2**

23. Evaluate the following:

Push(9)

Push(4)

Push(pop() + pop())

Push(4)

Push (pop() + pop())

Solution :

Push(9)	9	
Push(4)	9	4
Push(pop() + pop())	13	
Push(4)	13	4
Push (pop() + pop())	**17**	

24. Evaluate the following:

Push(9)

Push(41)

Push(pop() * pop())

Push(2)

Push (pop() + pop())

Solution :

Push(9)	9	
Push(41)	9	41
Push(pop() * pop())	369	
Push(2)	369	2
Push (pop() + pop())	**371**	

25. Evaluate the following:

Push(9)

Push(10)

Push(pop() * pop())

Push(2)

Push (pop() + pop())

Solution :

Push(9)	9	
Push(10)	9	10
Push(pop() * pop())	90	
Push(2)	90	2
Push (pop() + pop())	**92**	

26. Aqueue is a ________ (FIFO/LIFO). Fill in the blank.

Solution : FIFO (First in first out)

27. Evaluate the following

Push(2)

Push(9)

Push(pop() * pop())

Push(2)

Push (pop() - pop())

Solution :

Push(2)	2	
Push(9)	2	9
Push(pop() * pop())	18	
Push(2)	18	2
Push (pop() + pop())	16	

28. Evaluate the following

Push(12)

Push(10)

Push(pop() * pop())

Push(12)

Push (pop() + pop())

Push(10)

Push(pop() +pop())

Solution :

Push(12)	12	
Push(10)	12	10
Push(pop() * pop())	120	
Push(12)	120	12
Push (pop() + pop())	132	
Push(10)	132	10
Push(pop() +pop())	142	

29. What will be binary tree for: adeffsef ?

Solution :

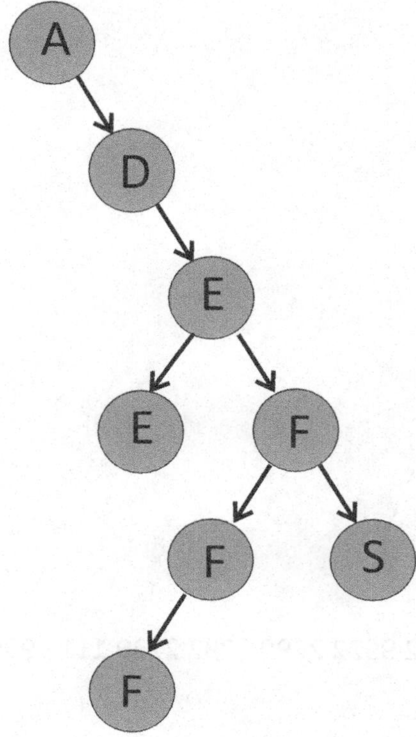

30. What will be the binary tree for " 10 12 21 21 12 10 " ?

Solution :

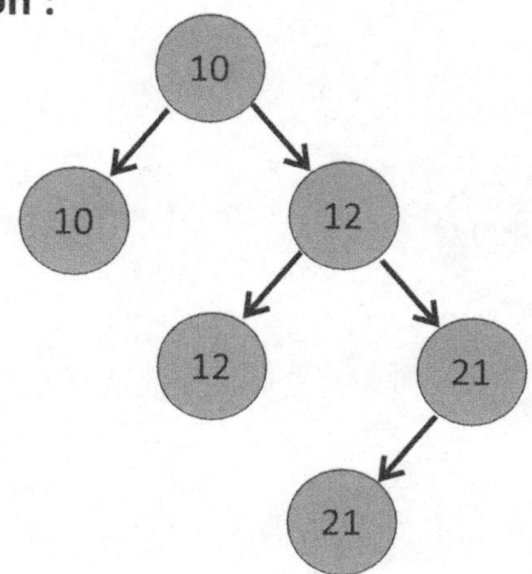

31. What will be the binary tree for " 123 321 223 332 213 231 " ?

Solution :

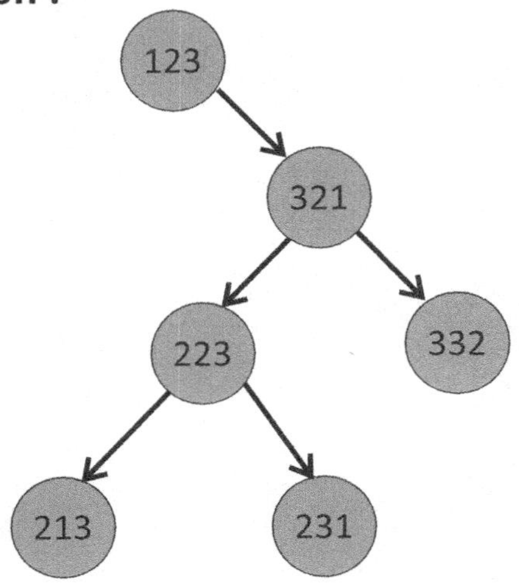

32. What will be the binary tree for " 2229 2992 9922 2299 2292 2229 1112 9992 " ?

Solution :

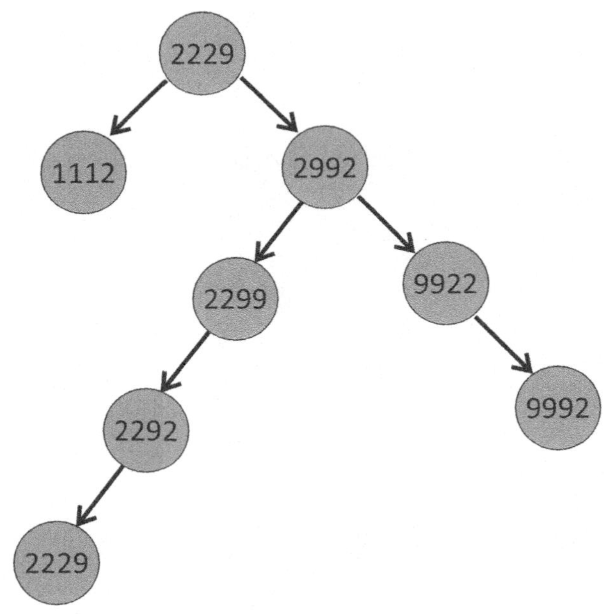

33. What will be the binary tree for " 212 112 121 221 210 201 102 120 100 120 " ?

Solution :

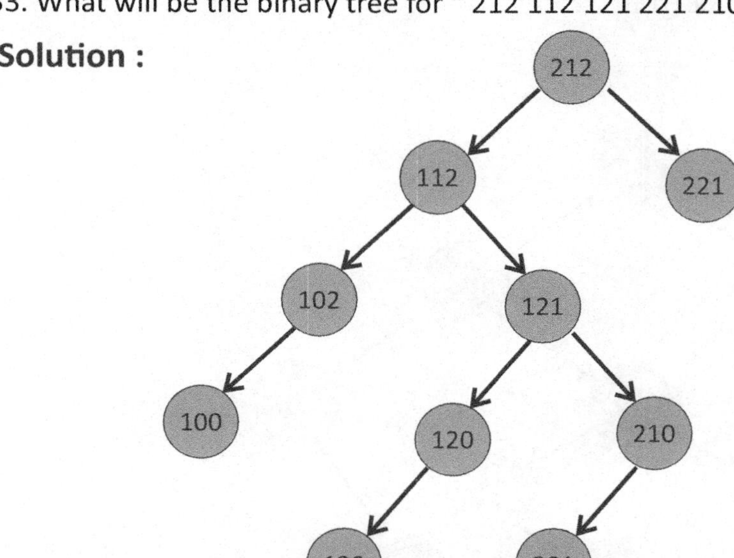

34. What will be the binary tree for " DROPDOWNMENU " ?

Solution :

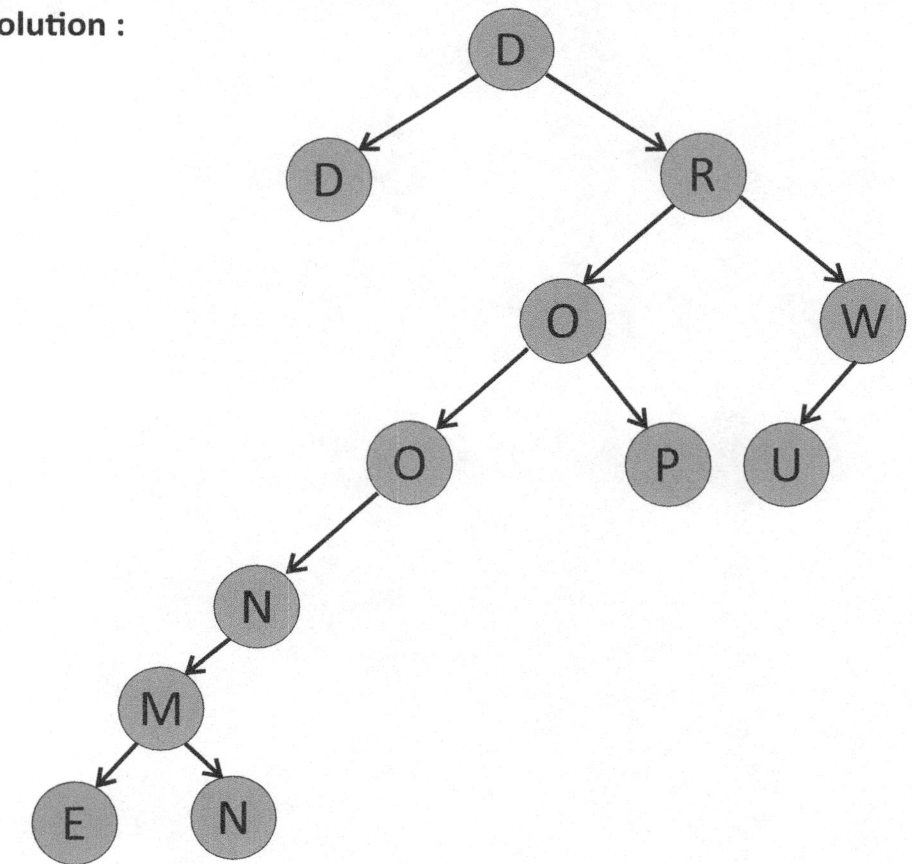

35. What will be the binary tree for " CROSSRICHTER " ?

Solution :

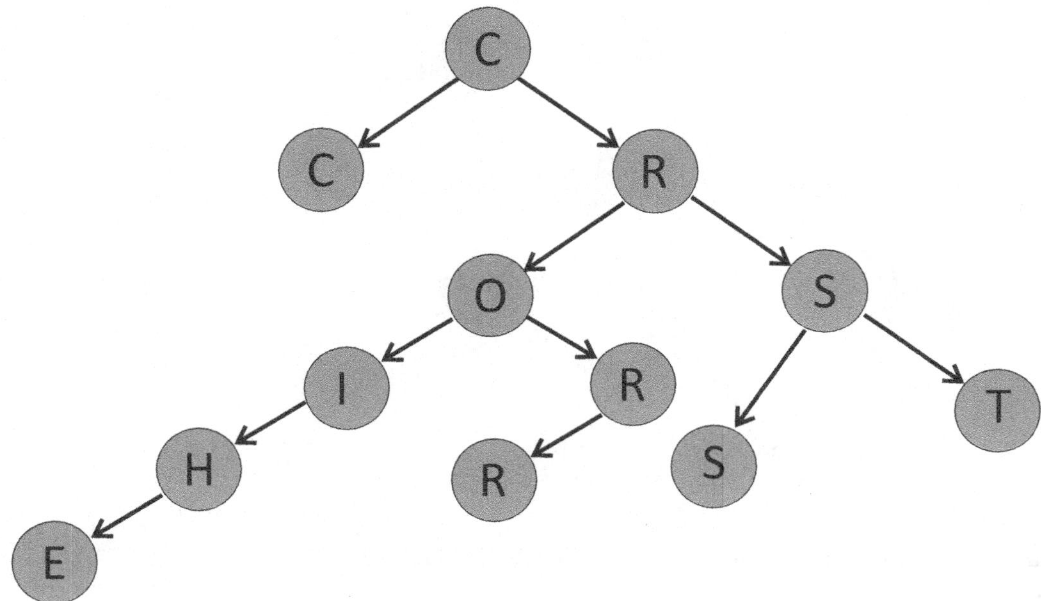

36. What will be the binary tree for " CREEKANDCRACK " ?

Solution :

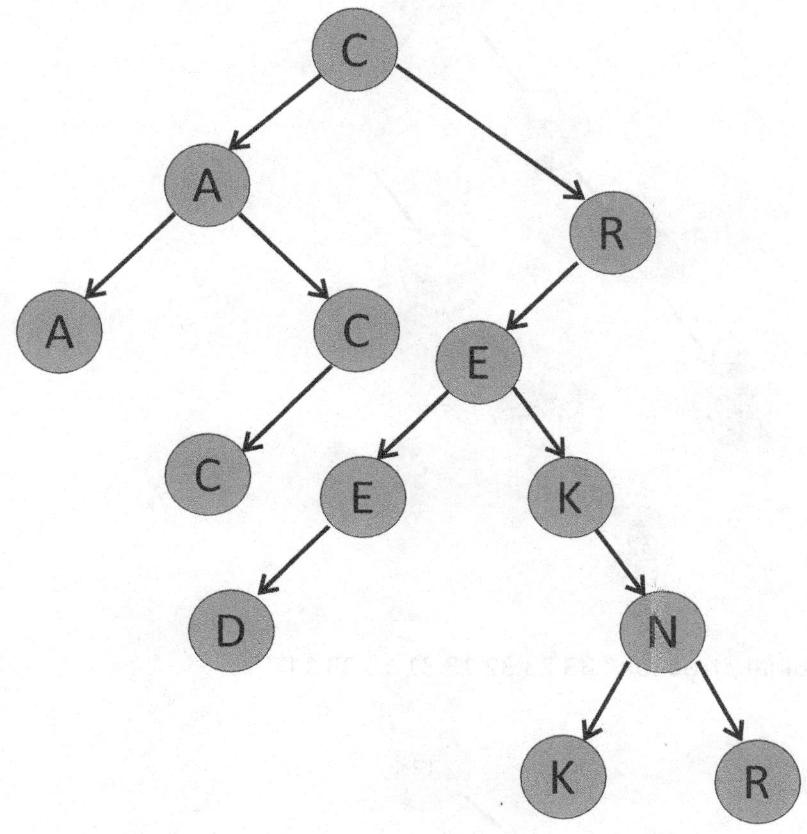

37. What will be the binary tree for " 123 321 123 321 123 321 123 321 " ?

Solution :

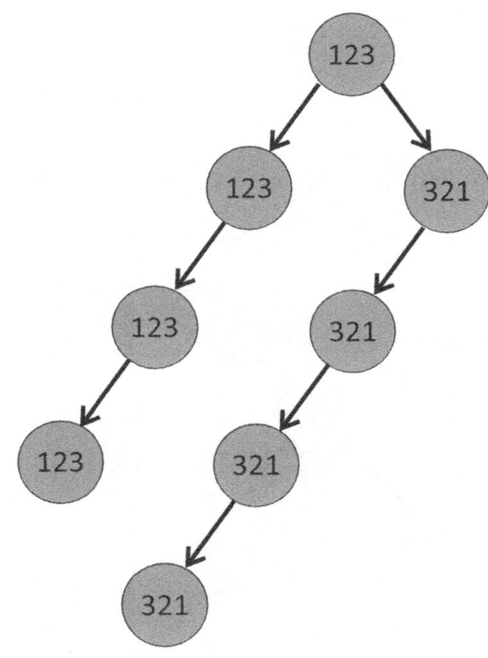

38. What will be the binary tree for " 33 23 32 13 31 13 33 11 " ?

Solution :

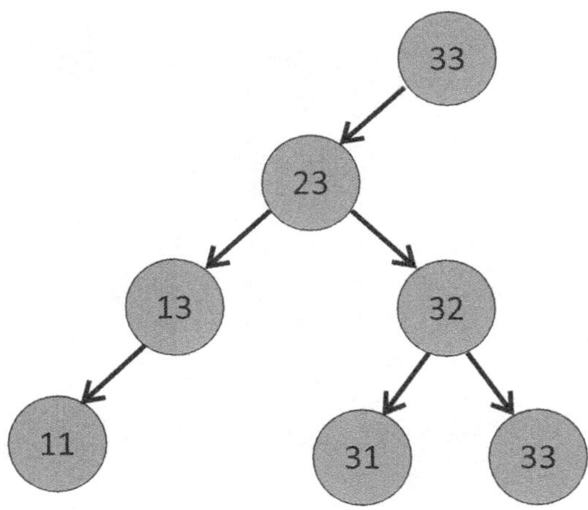

39. What will be the binary tree for " 93 99 100 3999 91 999 31 " ?

Solution :

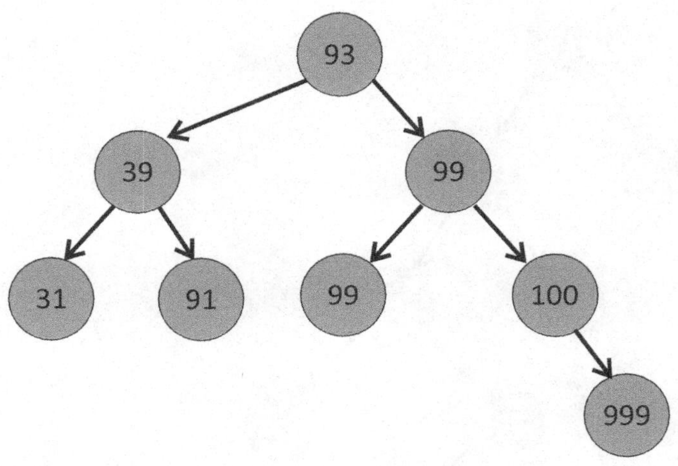

40. What will be the binary tree for " 144 441 414 441 141 411 414 114 411 " ?

Solution :

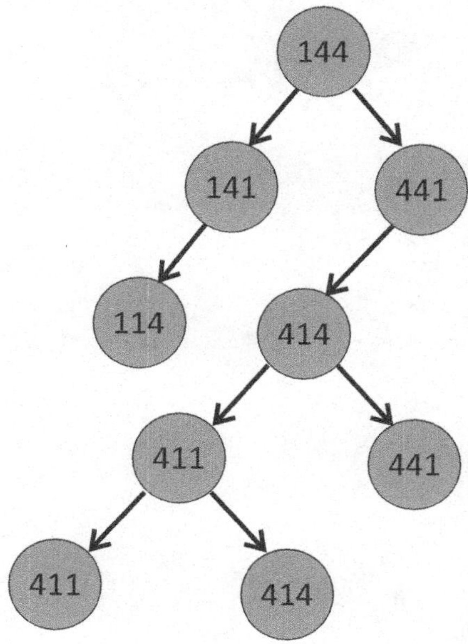

41. What will be the binary tree for " AFTERMARKETANALYSIS " ?

Solution :

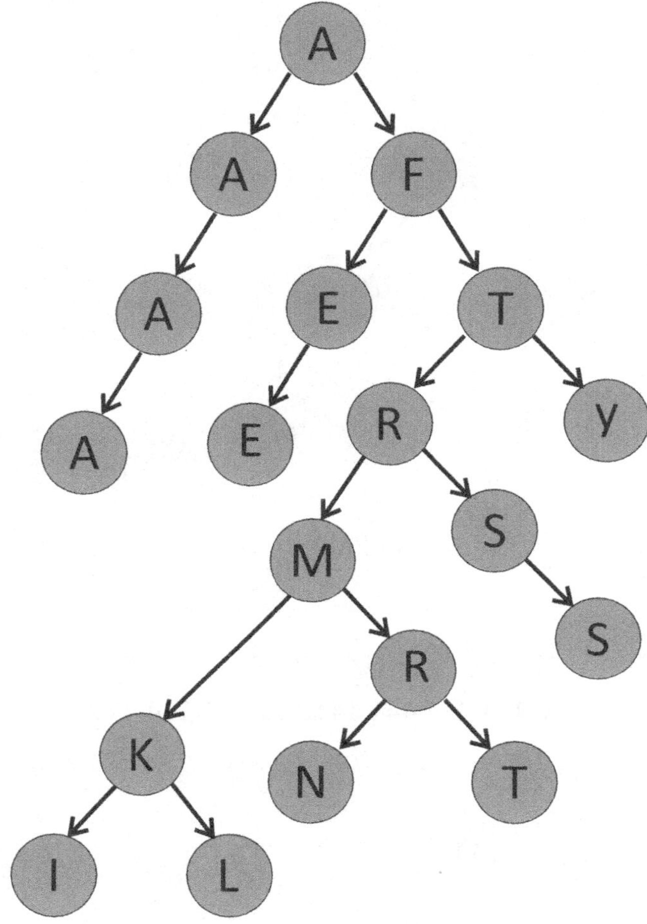

42. What will be the binary tree for " STACKSANDQUUS " ?

Solution :

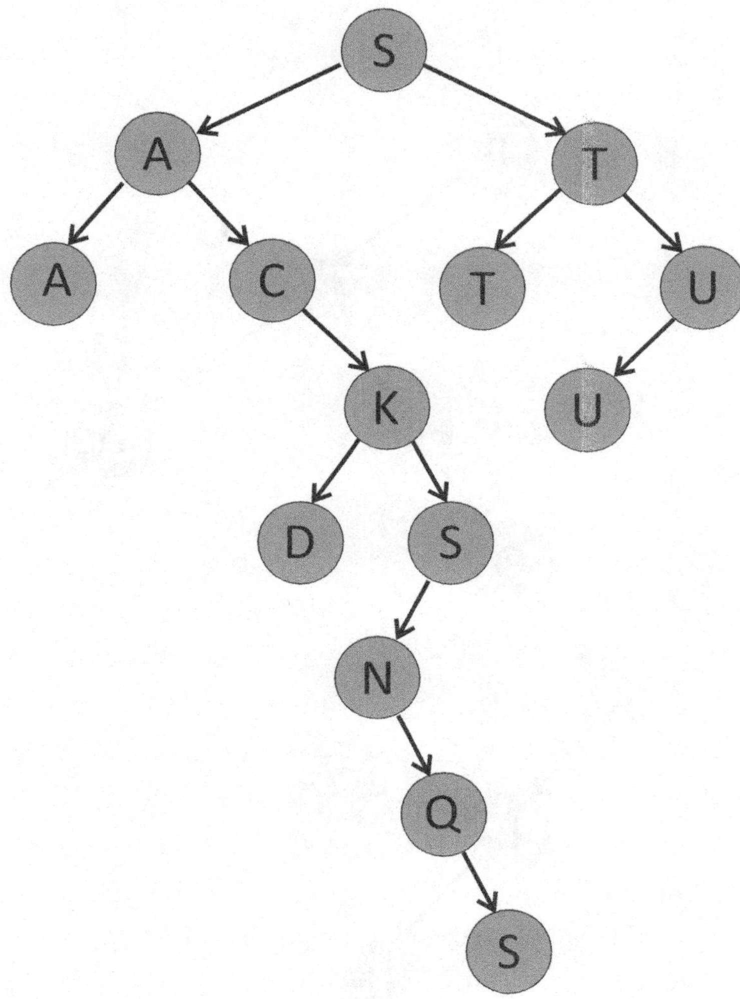

43. What will be the binary tree for " BROOKLYNNEWYORK " ?

Solution :

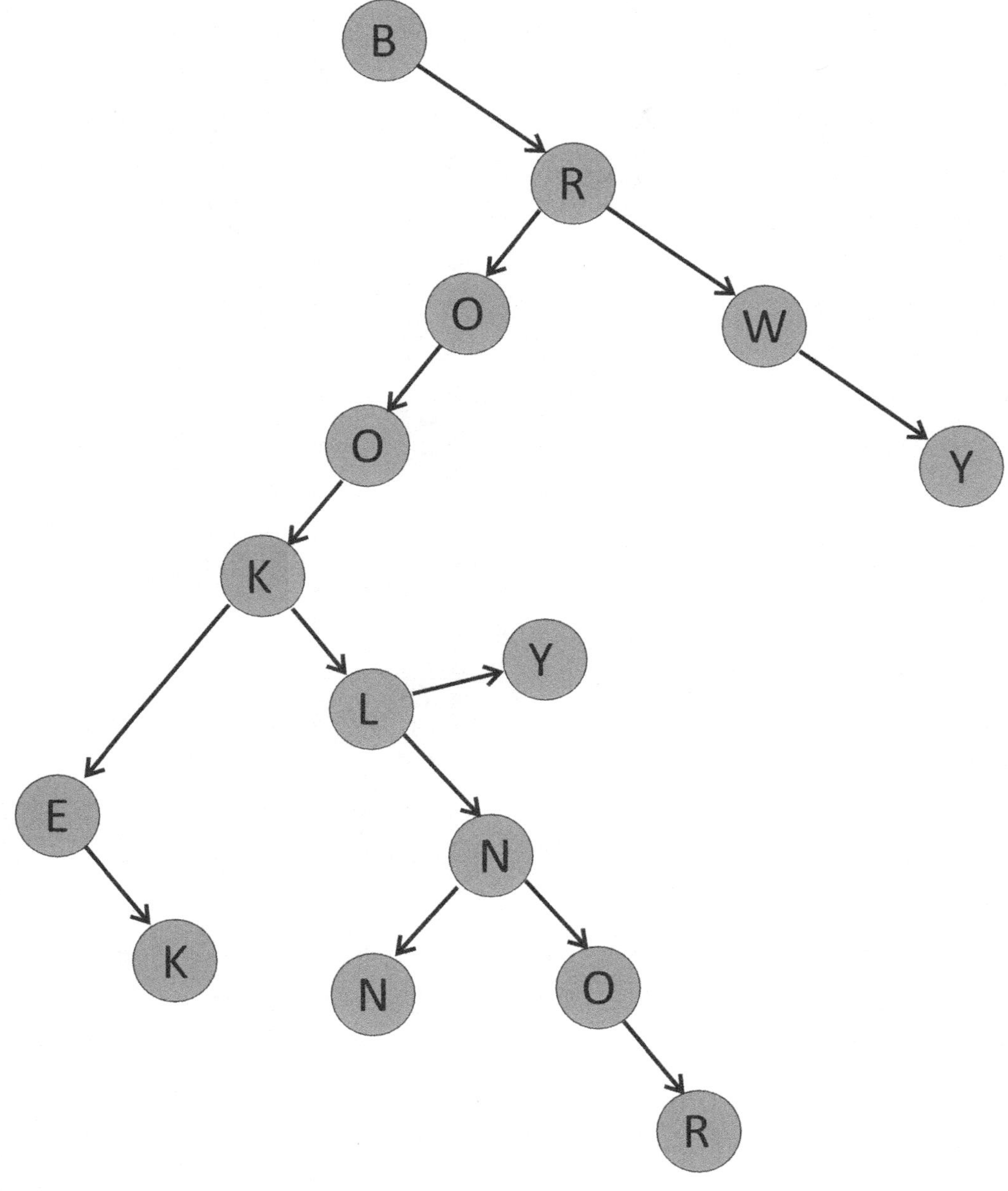

44. What will be the binary tree for " COMPUTERALGORITHM " ?

Solution :

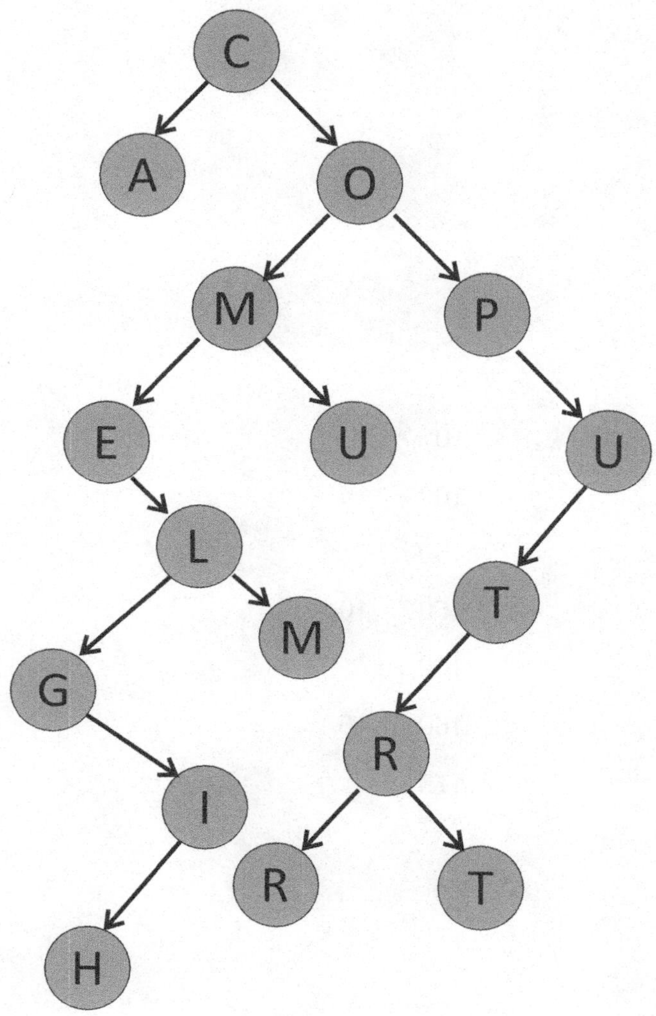

45. Evaluate the following expression:

Push(10)

Push(15)

Push(pop() * pop())

Push(10)

Push (pop() + pop())

Push(15)

Push(pop() +pop())

Solution :

Push(10)	10	
Push(15)	10	15
Push(pop() * pop())	150	
Push(10)	150	10
Push (pop() + pop())	160	
Push(15)	160	15
Push(pop() +pop())	175	

46. Evaluate the following expression:

Push(121)

Push(101)

Push(pop() + pop())

Push(111)

Push (pop() + pop())

Push(121)

Push(pop() +pop())

Solution :

Push(121)	121	
Push(101)	121	101
Push(pop() + pop())	222	
Push(111)	222	111
Push (pop() + pop())	333	
Push(121)	333	121
Push(pop() +pop())	454	

47. What will be the binary tree for " ABDOMINOUS " ?

Solution :

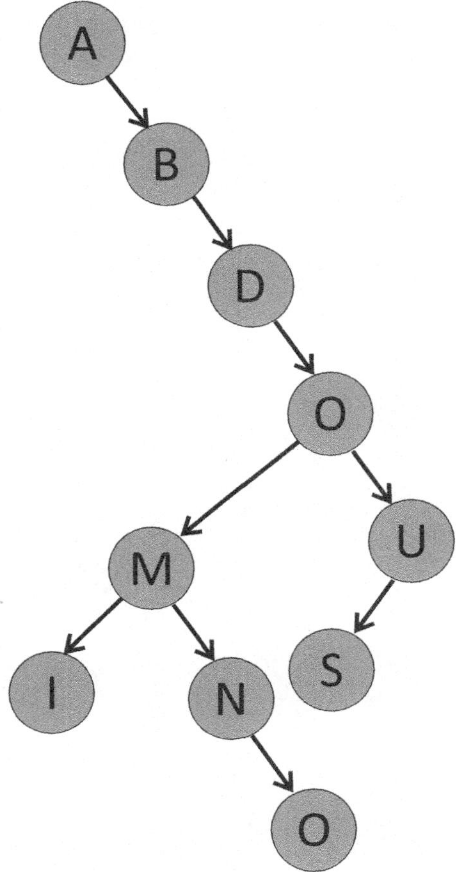

48. What will be the binary tree for " ADMEASUREMENT " ?

Solution :

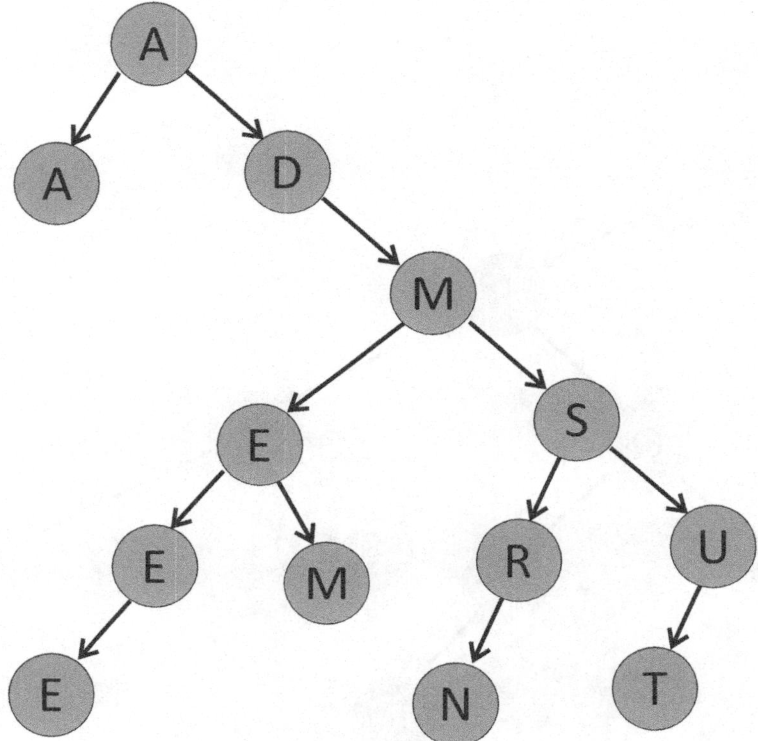

49. What will be the binary tree for " AKERATOPHOROUS " ?

Solution :

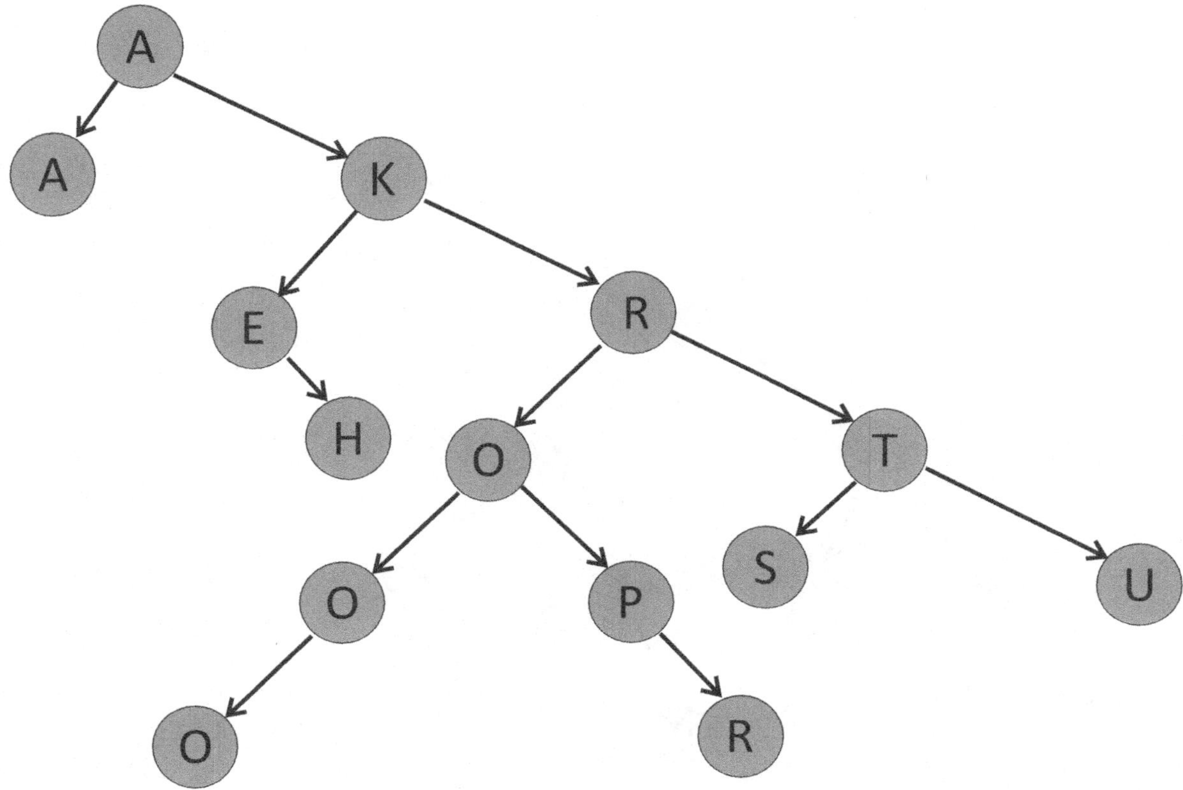

50. What will be the binary tree for " ANAESTHESIOLOGY " ?

Solution :

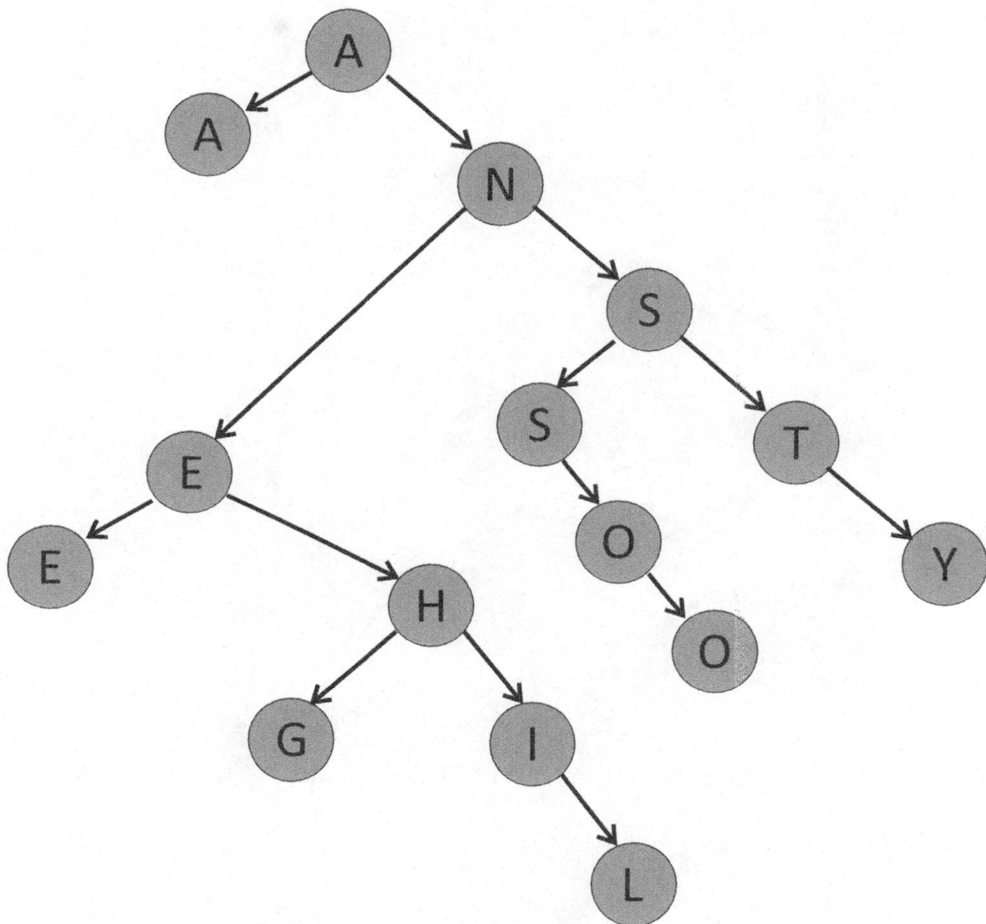

1. What is the output of the below program if the user enters i = 1 2 5 8 ?

```
int Arr[100],n,i,sum=0
        for(i=0;i<n;i++)
        sum+=Arr[i]

Output("\nThe sum of Array is :")<<sum
Output("\nThe average of Array is :")<<sum/i

}
```

Output:
The sum of Array is : 16
The average of Array is : 4

2. What is the output of the below program i = 16 10 12 12 14 15 ?

```
{
        int Arr[5],n,i,temp
        temp=Arr[0]
        Arr[0]=Arr[n-1]
        Arr[n-1]=temp
        Output("\nArray after swapping")<<endl
        for(i=0;i<n;i++)
                Output(Arr[i])
}
```

Output:

Array after swapping 15 10 12 12 14 16

3. What is the output of the below program ?
if the number of elements is 4 and the elements are i = 4 5 8 2 9?

```
{
        Input Arr[100],n,temp,i,j
        for(i=0;j=n-1;i<n/2;i++;j--)
        {
                temp=Arr[i]
                Arr[i]=Arr[j]
                Arr[j]=temp
        }
        Output("\n array")<<endl
        for(i=0 i<n i++)
      Output(Arr[i])


}
```

Output:
array
9 2 8 5 4

4. What is the output of the below program
if the elements entered are 5 and the elements are i= 9 8 7 3 5 2 ?

```
        int Arr[100],n,i,small,large
        small=Arr[0]
        large=Arr[0]
        for(i=1;i<n;i++)
        {
                if(Arr[i]<small)
                        small=Arr[i]
                if(Arr[i]>large)
                        large=Arr[i]
        }

        Output("\nelement is :")<<large
        Output("\nelement is :")<<small

}
```

Output:
element is : 9
element is : 2

5. What is the output of the program if the elements are 9 10 11 8 10 3 ?

```
{
Int b[5],I,b=0, n=10
Output("Enter the array:")
for(i=0;i<n;i++)
{
Input a[i]
if(a[i]>=10)
b++
}
Output("The number of integers greater or equal to 10 is: ")<<b
}
```

Output:
The number of integers greater or equal to 10 is : 2

6. What is the output of the below program ?

```
for x = 1:3
 for y = 1:3
   if x==y
     z(x,y) = 1
   elseif x < y
      z(x,y) = 0
   else
      z(x,y) = 1
   end
 end
end
```

Output:

```
1  0  0
1  1  0
1  1  1
```

7. What is the output of the below program ?

```
for x = 1:3
 for y = 1:3
    if x==y
      z(x,y) = 2
    elseif x < y
       z(x,y) = 0
    else
       z(x,y) = 2
    end
  end
end
```

Output:

```
2  0  0
2  2  0
2  2  2
```

8. What is the output of the below program ?

```
z = zeros(4)
for x = 1:3
 for y = 1:3
    if x==y
      z(x,y) = x^2 + y^2
    elseif x < y
       z(x,y) = 0
    else
       z(x,y) = x-y
    end
  end
end
```

Output:

```
2  0   0
1  8   0
2  1  18
```

9. What is the output of the below program ?

```
for x = 1:3
 for y = 1:3
    if x==y
      z(x,y) = x + y
    elseif x < y
       z(x,y) = x
    else
       z(x,y) = y - x
    end
  end
end
```

Output:

```
 2   1  1
-1   4  2
-2  -1  6
```

10. What is the output of the below program ?

```
for x = 1:3
 for y = 1:3
    if x==y
      z(x,y) = y
    elseif x < y
       z(x,y) = y
    else
       z(x,y) = -x
    end
  end
end
```

Output:

```
 1   2   3
-2   2   3
-3  -3   3
```

11. What is the output of the below program ?

```
for x = 1:3
 for y = 1:3
    if x==y
      z(x,y) = y
    elseif x < y
       z(x,y) = y*y
    else
       z(x,y) = x*x
    end
  end
end
```

Output :

```
1  4  9
4  2  9
9  9  3
```

12. What is the output of the below program ?

```
for x = 1:4
 for y = 1:4
    if x==y
      z(x,y) = x^2 - y^2
    elseif x < y
       z(x,y) = y
    else
       z(x,y) = x
    end
  end
end
```

Output :

```
0  2  3  4
2  0  3  4
3  3  0  4
4  4  4  0
```

13. What is the output of the below program ?

```
for x = 1:4
 for y = 1:4
    if x==y
      z(x,y) = x^2
    elseif x < y
       z(x,y) = y
    else
       z(x,y) = y^2
    end
 end
end
```

Output :

```
1  2  3  4
1  4  3  4
1  4  9  4
1  4  9 16
```

14. What is the output of the below program ?

```
z = zeros(4)

for x = 1:4
 for y = 1:4
    if x==y
      z(x,y) = y/x
    elseif x < y
       z(x,y) = y
    else
       z(x,y) = x/y
    end
 end
end
```

Output :

```
1.0000  2.0000  3.0000  4.0000
2.0000  1.0000  3.0000  4.0000
3.0000  1.5000  1.0000  4.0000
4.0000  2.0000  1.3333  1.0000
```

15. What is the output of the below program ?

```
z = 0.0000

for x = 1:4
 for y = 1:4
    if x==y
      z(x,y) = y/x
    elseif x < y
      z(x,y) = y^2
    else
      z(x,y) = x/y
    end
  end
end
```

Output :

```
1.0000  4.0000  9.0000  16.0000
2.0000  1.0000  9.0000  16.0000
3.0000  1.5000  1.0000  16.0000
4.0000  2.0000  1.3333   1.0000
```

16. What is the output of the below program ?

```
for x = 1:4
 for y = 1:4
    if x==y
      z(x,y) = x^2
    else
      z(x,y) = y^x
    end
  end
end
```

Output :

```
1  4  9  16
1  4  9  16
1  4  9  16
1  4  9  0
```

17. What is the output of the below program ?

```
for x = 1:4
 for y = 1:4
    if x==y
      z(x,y) = x^2
    else
       z(x,y) = y^x
    end
  end
end
```

Output :

```
 1   2   3   4
 1   4   9  16
 1   8   9  64
 1  16  81   0
```

18. What is the output of the below program ?

```
for x = 1:4
 for y = 1:4
    if x==y
      z(x,y) = x^2
    else
       z(x,y) = x^2 + y^2

    end
  end
end
```

Output :

```
  1   5  10  17
  5   4  13  20
 10  13   9  25
 17  20  25  16
```

19. What is the output of the below program ?

```
for x = 1:4
 for y = 1:4
    if x==y
      z(x,y) = x^2
    else
       z(x,y) = 2*y
    end
  end
end
 Output(z)
```

Output :

```
 1  2  6   8
 2  4  6   8
 2  4  9   8
 2  4  6  16
```

20. What is the output of the below program ?

```
for x = 1:4
 for y = 1:4
    if x==y
      z(x,y) = x^2
    elseif x < y
       z(x,y) = x^2
    else
      z(x,y) = y^2
    end
  end
end
 Output (z)
```

Output :

```
1   1   1   1
1   4   4   4
1   4   9   9
1   4   9  16
```

21. What is the output below program ?

```
for x = 1:4
 for y = 1:4
    if x==y
      z(x,y) = x + y
    elseif x < y
       z(x,y) = x^2
    else
      z(x,y) = y + x
    end
  end
end
 Output (z)
```

Output :

```
2   1   1   1
3   4   4   4
4   5   6   9
5   6   7   8
```

22. What is the output of the below program ?

```
for x = 1:4
 for y = 1:4
    if x==y
      z(x,y) = x + y
    elseif x < y
       z(x,y) = x*y
    else
      z(x,y) = y + x
    end
 end
end
 Output (z)
```

Output :

```
2  2  3  4
3  4  6  8
4  5  6  12
5  6  7  8
```

23. What is the output of the below program ?

```
for x = 1:4
 for y = 1:4
    if x==y
      z(x,y) = x+y
    elseif x < y
       z(x,y) = x*y
    else
      z(x,y) = y*x
    end
 end
end
 Output (z)
```

Output :

```
2  2  3  4
2  4  6  8
3  6  6  12
4  8  12  8
```

24. What is the output of the below program ?

```
for x = 1:4
 for y = 1:4
    if x==y
      z(x,y) = x/y
    elseif x < y
       z(x,y) = x*x
    else
      z(x,y) = y*x
    end
 end
end
 Output (z)
```

Output :

```
1  1  1  1
2  1  4  4
3  6  1  9
4  8  12  1
```

25. What is the output of the below program ?

```
for x = 1:4
 for y = 1:4
    if x==y
      z(x,y) = x*y
    elseif x < y
       z(x,y) = x*x
    else
      z(x,y) = y*y
    end
 end
end
 Output (z)
```

Output :

```
1  1  1  1
1  4  4  4
1  4  9  9
1  4  9 16
```

26. What is the output of the below program ?

```
z = 0.0000

for x = 1:4
 for y = 1:4
    if x==y
      z(x,y) = x/y
    elseif x < y
       z(x,y) = x/x
    else
      z(x,y) = y/x
    end
 end
end
 Output (z)
```

Output :

```
1.0000  1.0000  1.0000  1.0000
0.5000  1.0000  1.0000  1.0000
0.3333  0.6667  1.0000  1.0000
0.2500  0.5000  0.7500  1.0000
```

27. What is the output of the below program ?

```
A = 100
B = 10
z = 0.0000
for x = 1:3
 for y = 1:3
    if x<y
      z(x,y) = sqrt(A)
    elseif x > y
       z(x,y) = sqrt(B)
    else
       z(x,y) = sqrt(A+B)
    end
  end
end
Output (z)
```

Output :

```
10.4881  10.0000  10.0000
 3.1623  10.4881  10.0000
 3.1623   3.1623  10.4881
```

28. What is the output of the below program ?

```
A = 10
B = 10
z = 0.0000

for x = 1:3
 for y = 1:3
    if x<y
      z(x,y) = √A
    elseif x > y
       z(x,y) = √B
    else
       z(x,y) = √(A/B)
    end
  end
end
Output(z)
```

Output :

```
1.0000  3.1623  3.1623
3.1623  1.0000  3.1623
3.1623  3.1623  1.0000
```

29. What is the output of the below program ?

```
A = 8
B = 10
z = 0.0000

for x = 1:3
 for y = 1:3
   if x < y
     z(x,y) = sqrt(A*B)
   elseif x > y
      z(x,y) = sqrt(B)
   else
      z(x,y) = sqrt( A/B )
   end
 end
end
Output(z)
```

Output :

```
0.8944  8.9443  8.9443
3.1623  0.8944  8.9443
3.1623  3.1623  0.8944
```

30. What is the output of the below program ?

```
A = 121
B = 121


for x = 1:5
 for y = 1:5
   if x<y
     z(x,y) = sqrt( A/B )
   elseif x > y
      z(x,y) = sqrt( B/A )
   else
      z(x,y) = sqrt( A/B )
   end
 end
end
Output(z)
```

Output :

```
1  1  1  1  1
1  1  1  1  1
1  1  1  1  1
1  1  1  1  1
1  1  1  1  1
```

31. What is the output of the below program ?

```
A = 5
B = 5

for x = 1:3
 for y = 1:3
   if x<y
     z(x,y) = sqrt(A*B)
   elseif x > y
      z(x,y) = sqrt( B/A )
   else
      z(x,y) = B
   end
  end
end
Output(z)
```

Output :

```
5  5  5
1  5  5
1  1  5
```

32. What is the output of the below program ?

```
A = 9
B = 25

for x = 1:3
 for y = 1:3
   if x<y
     z(x,y) = sqrt(A*B)
   elseif x > y
      z(x,y) = sqrt(B)
   else
      z(x,y) = B
   end
  end
end
Output(z)
```

Output :

```
25  15  15
 5  25  15
 5   5   5
```

33. What is the output of the below program 3 5 6 2 4 ?

```
{
            int Arr[100],n,i,s=0
}           for(i=0;i<n;i++)
                        sum+=Arr[i]

            Output(s)
}
```

Output:
4

34. What is the output of the below program ?

```
A = 3
B = 5

for x = 1:3
 for y = 1:3
    if x < y
      z(x,y) = sqrt(B)
    elseif x > y
       z(x,y) = A + B
    else
       z(x,y) = B
    end
  end
end
Output(z)
```

Output:

```
  5.0000   2.2361   2.2361
  8.0000   5.0000   2.2361
  8.0000   8.0000   5.0000
```

35. What is the output of the below program ?

```
A = 3
B = 3

for x = 1:3
 for y = 1:3
    if x < y
      z(x,y) = sqrt(B)
    elseif x > y
       z(x,y) = B^2
    else
       z(x,y) = B
    end
  end
end
Output(z)
```

Output :

```
  3.0000   1.7321   1.7321
  9.0000   3.0000   1.7321
  9.0000   9.0000   3.0000
```

36. What is the output of the below program ?

```
A = 5
B = 5

for x = 1:3
 for y =1:3
   if x<y
     z(x,y) = B*2
   elseif x > y
       z(x,y) = B^2
   else
       z(x,y) = A^2
   end
 end
end
Output(z)
```

Output :

```
25  10  10
25  25  10
25  25  25
```

37. What is the output of the below program ?

```
A = 9
B = 14

for x = 1:3
 for y = 1:3
   if x < y
     z(x,y) = B/A
   elseif x > y
       z(x,y) = B-A
   else
       z(x,y) = A+B
   end
 end
end
Output(z)
```

Output :

```
21   2   2
 7  21   2
 7   7  21
```

38. What is the output of the below program ?

```
A = 4
B = 4

for x = 1:4
 for y = 1:4
    if x < y
      z(x,y) = A^2
    elseif x > y
      z(x,y) = B^2
    else
      z(x,y) = A + B
    end
  end
end
Output(z)
```

Output :

```
 8  16  16  16
16   8  16  16
16  16   8  16
16  16  16   8
```

39. What is the output of the below program ?

```
A = 4
B = 4

for x = 1:4
 for y = 1:4
    if x < y
      z(x,y) = A/2
    elseif x > y
      z(x,y) = B*2

    else
      z(x,y) = (A + B)/2
    end
  end
end
Output(z)
```

Output :

```
4  2  2  2
8  4  2  2
8  8  4  2
8  8  8  4
```

40. What is the output of the below program ?

```
for x = 1:3
 for y = 1:3
    if x==y
      z(x,y) = 0
    elseif x < y
       z(x,y) = 5
    else
       z(x,y) = 7
    end
  end
end
```

Output :

```
0  5  5  5  5
7  0  5  5  5
7  7  0  5  5
7  7  7  0  5
7  7  7  7  0
```

41) In the array X given as below with X(1,1) = 4,
what is the output of the below program ?

```
FOR I = 1 TO 4
    FOR J = 1 TO 4
        IF X(I,J)/5 = INT ( X(I,J)/5 )
                THEN X(I,J) = X(I,J)/5
        ELSE X(I,J) = X(I,J) - 1
        IF X(I,J) < 0
                THEN X(I,J) = (ABS(X(I,J)))/5
        ELSE X(I,J) = 2 * X(I,J)
    NEXT J
NEXT I
END
```

-4	20	30	40
20	-9	30	40
20	30	-14	40
20	30	40	-19

Output :

1	-8	-12	-16
-8	2	-12	-16
-8	-12	3	-16
-8	-12	-16	4

42) In the array X given as below with X(1,1) = 2,

what is the output of the below program ?

2	-2	-4
-2	2	-2
-4	-2	2

```
S = 0
    FOR I = 1 TO 3
        FOR J = 1 TO 3
            IF X(I,J) = INT (X(I,J))
                THEN X(I,J) = X(I,J)*2
            ELSE X(I,J) = X(I,J) + 2
            IF X(I,J) < 0
                THEN X(I,J) = (ABS(X(I,J))) *2
            ELSE X(I,J)  =  2 * X(I,J)
           S = S + X(I,J)
        NEXT J
    NEXT I
    END
    PRINT S
```

Output :

-8	0	4
0	-8	0
4	0	-8

S = -16

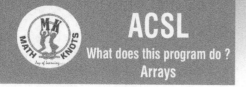

43. What is the output of the below program ?

```
for I = 1 to 4
        for J = 1 to 4
                A(I,J) = 2 * I
                B(I,J) = 3 * J
                C(I,J) = A(I,J) + B(J,I)
        next J
next I
end
```

Output :

A =

2	2	2	2
4	4	4	4
6	6	6	6
8	8	8	8

B =

3	3	3	3
6	6	6	6
9	9	9	9
12	12	12	12

C =

5	5	5	5
10	10	10	10
15	15	15	15
20	20	20	20

44. What is the output of the below program ?

```
for i = 1 to 3
        for j = 1 to 3
                A(I,J) = i * i + j * j
                B(I,J) = j * j - i * i
                C(I,J) = A(I,J) - B(J,I)
        next J
next I
end
```

Output :

A =

2	5	10
5	8	13
10	13	18

B =

0	3	8
-3	0	5
-8	-5	0

C =

2	2	2
8	8	8
18	18	18

45. In the array X given as below with X(1,1) = -5,

    what is the output of the below program ?

-5	-5	-10
10	5	-5
5	10	-5

```
FOR I = 1 TO 3
    FOR J = 1 TO 3
        IF X(I,J)/5 = INT ( X(I,J)/5 )
            THEN X(I,J) = X(I,J)/5
        ELSE X(I,J) = X(I,J) - 5
        IF X(I,J) < 0
            THEN X(I,J) = (ABS(X(I,J)))*(-1)
        ELSE X(I,J) =  5 * X(I,J)
    NEXT J
NEXT I
END
```

Output :

10	10	15
-10	-5	10
-5	-10	10

1. How many paths of length 2 exist in the graph.

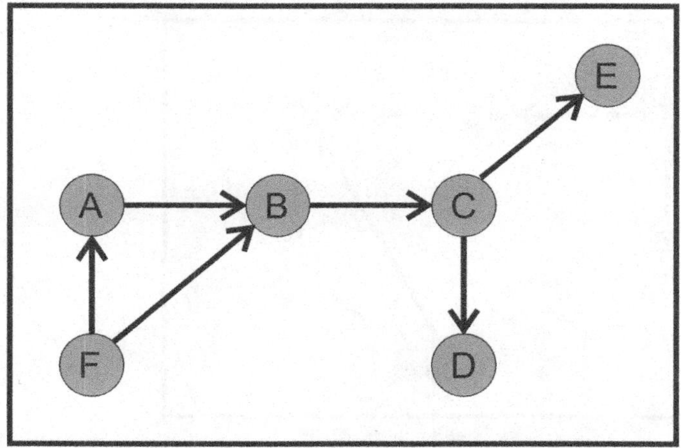

Solution:

5

2. What are the cyclic closed paths in this graph?

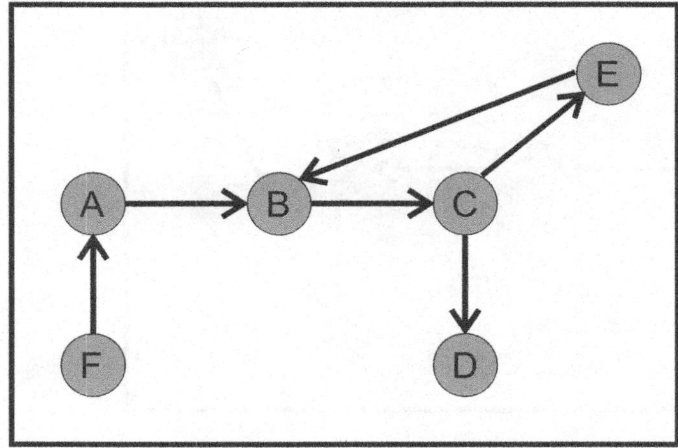

Solution:

BCEB

3. What are the closed cyclic paths in this graph?

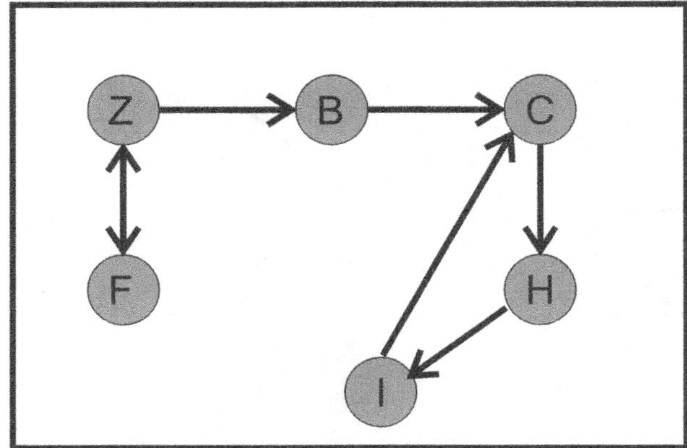

Solution:

CHIC, ZFZ

4. What is the adjacency atrix of the graph?

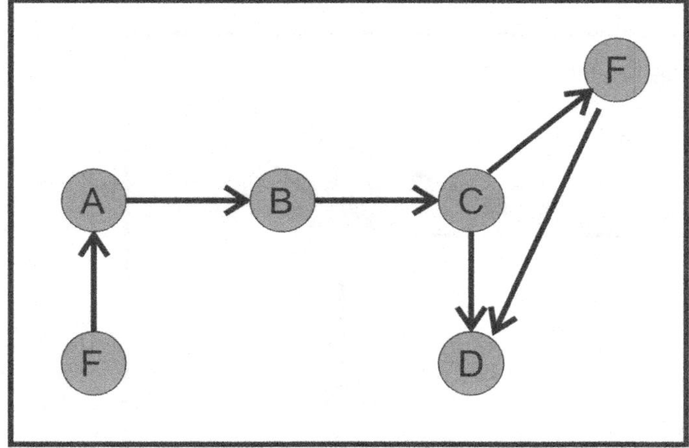

Solution:

	A	B	C	D	E	F
A	0	1	0	0	0	0
B	0	0	1	0	0	0
C	0	0	0	0	1	0
D	0	0	0	0	0	0
E	0	0	0	1	0	0
F	1	0	0	0	0	0

5. What are the cycles in this graph?

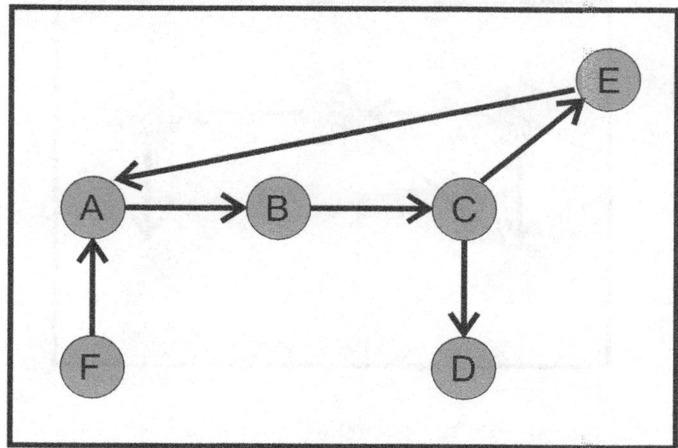

Solution:

ABCEA

6. How many paths with length 2 exist in the graph?

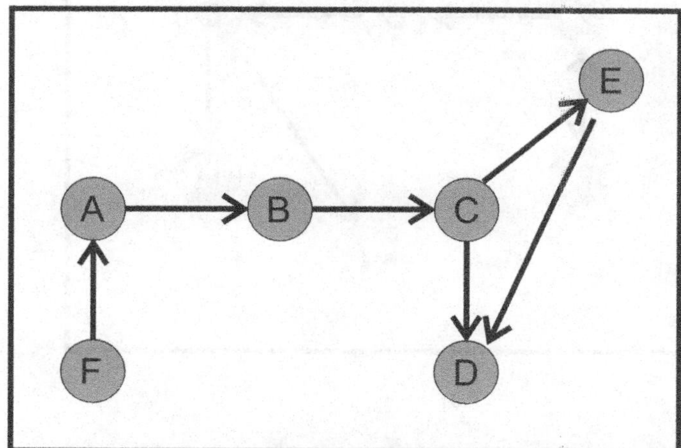

Solution:

4

7. What are the cycles in the graph?

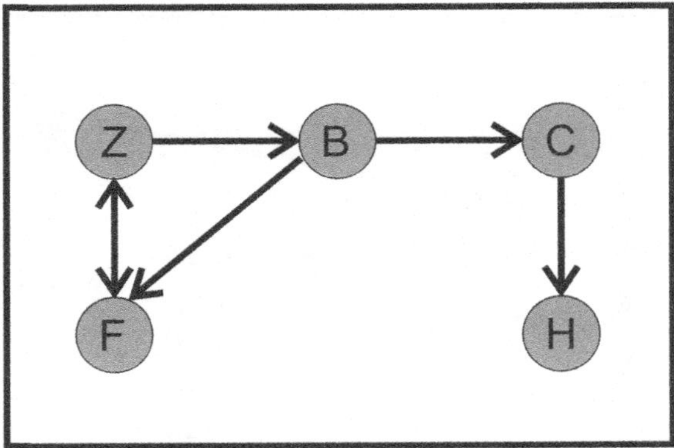

Solution:

ZBFZ, ZFZ

8. What are the cycles in the graph?

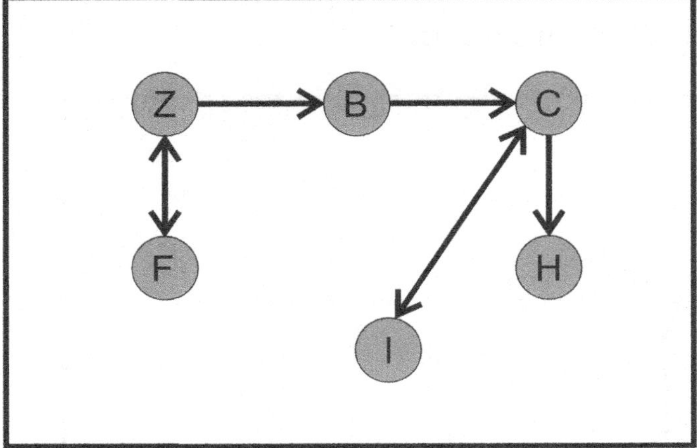

Solution:

ZFZ, CIC

9. What are the cycles in the graph?

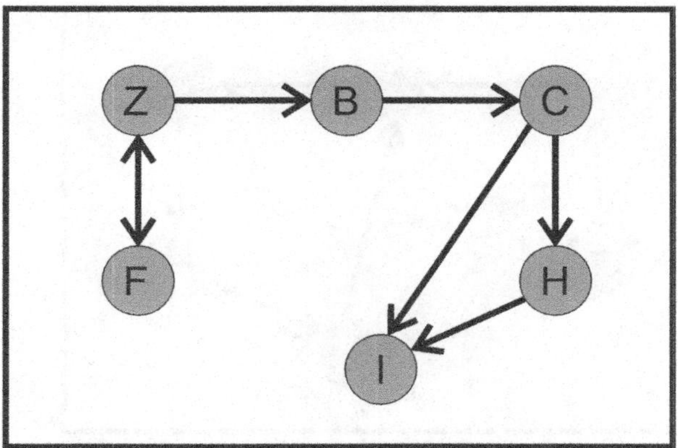

Solution:

ZFZ

10. What are the cycles in the graph?

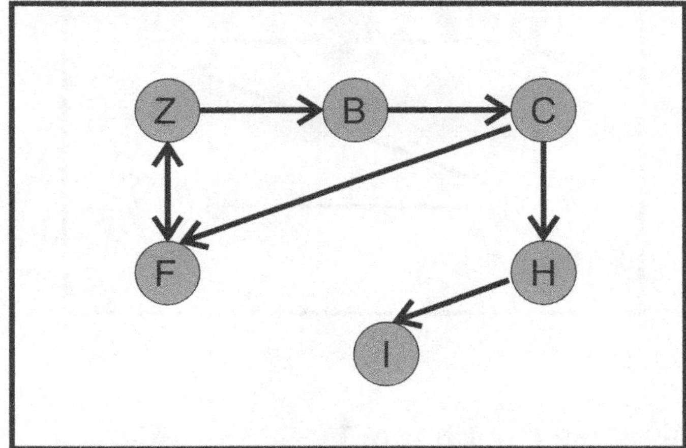

Solution:

ZBCFZ, ZFZ

11. What are the cycles in the graph?

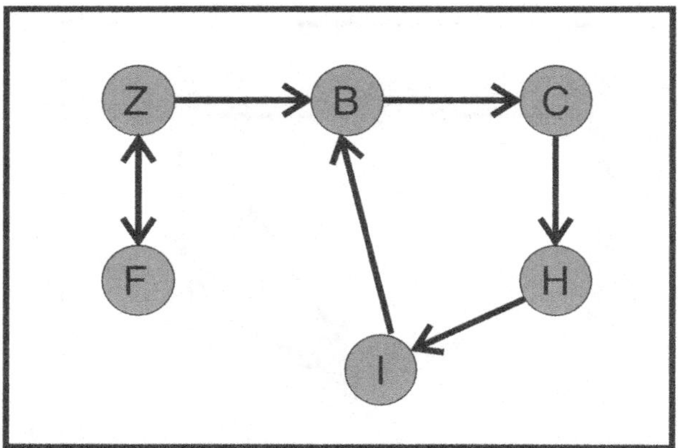

Solution:

BCHIB, ZFZ

12. Draw the graph for the following:

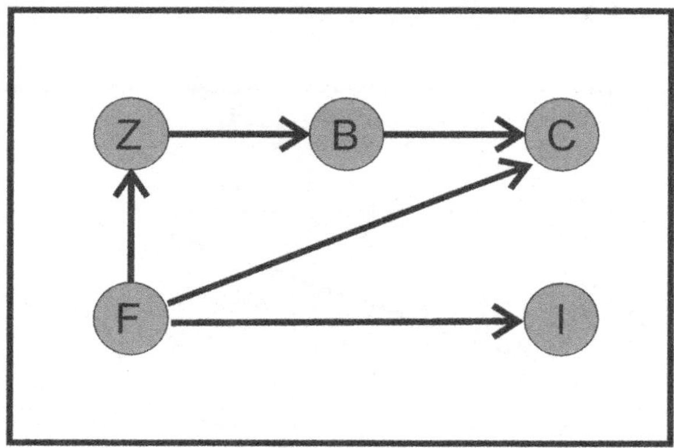

Solution:

	B	C	I	F	Z
B	0	1	0	0	0
C	0	0	0	0	0
I	0	0	0	0	0
F	0	1	0	0	1
Z	1	0	0	0	0

13. What are the cycles in the graph?

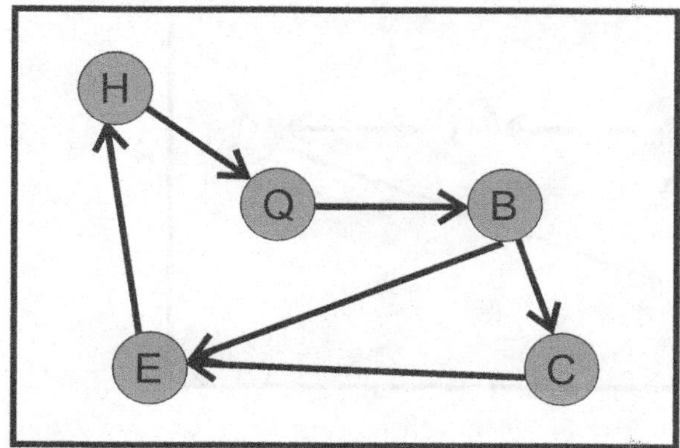

Solution:

HQBCEH, BCEB

14. How many paths of length 2 exist in graph?

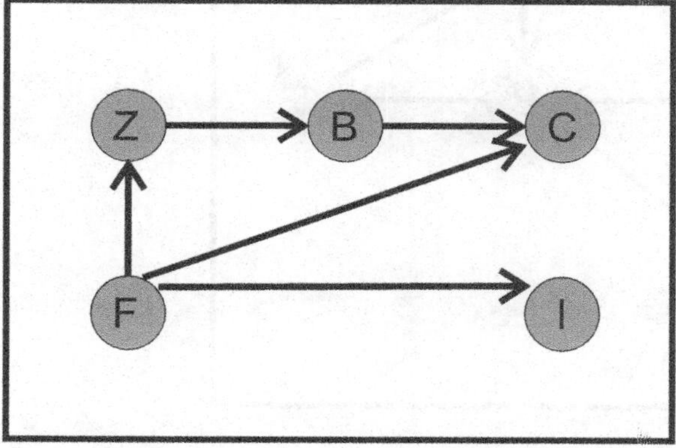

Solution:

ZBC,FZB

15. Is the graph cyclic? Justify?

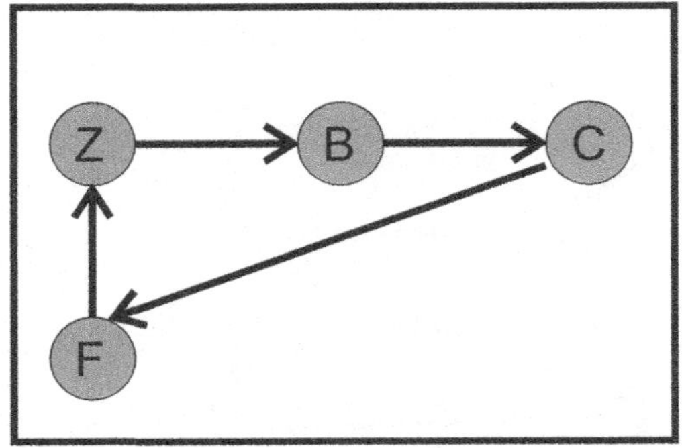

Solution:

ZBCFZ

16. Is there any cycle in this graph?

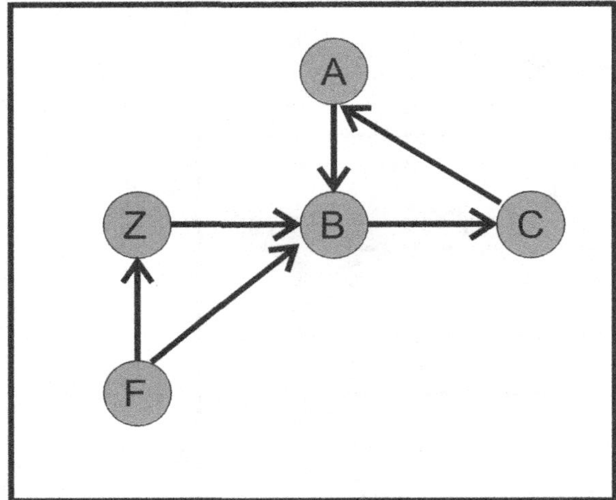

Solution:

BCAB

17. How many paths with length 2 in the graph?

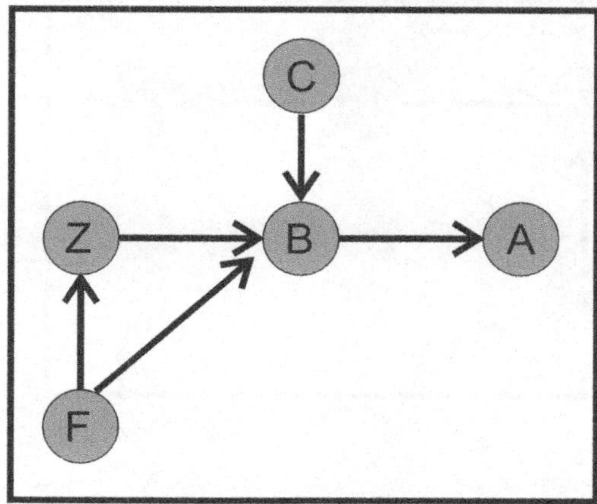

Solution:

3

CBA , ZBA , FBA

18. Is there a cyclic closed path in this graph?

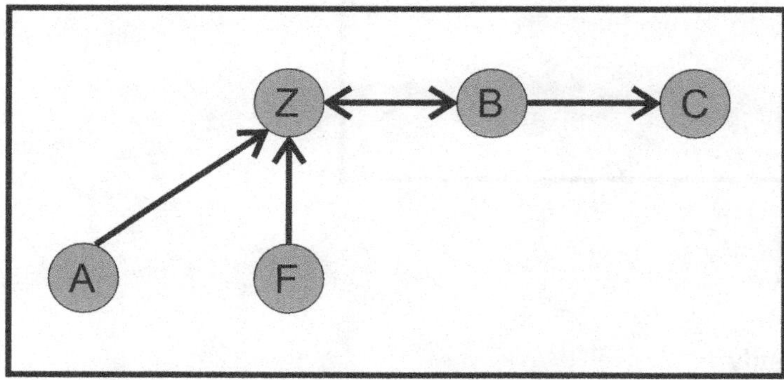

Solution:

ZBZ

19. How many paths of length 2 exist in the graph?

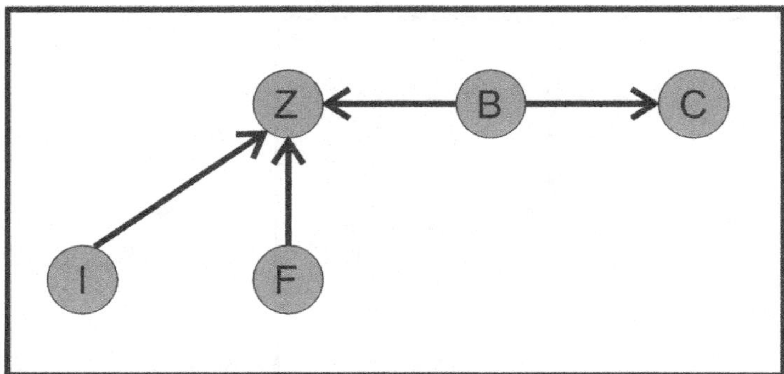

Solution:

0

20. Is this graph a closed graph?

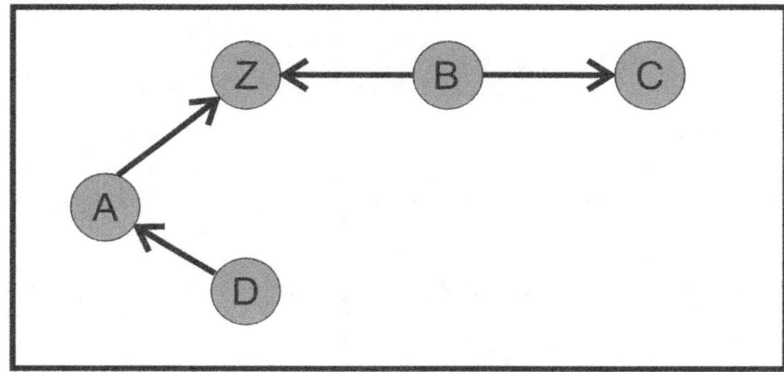

Solution:

No

21. Is the graph a closed graph? Justify

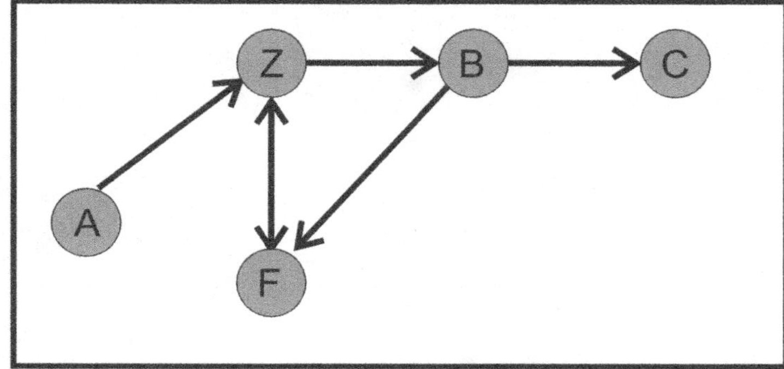

Solution:

ZBFZ, ZFZ

22. What are the cycles in the graph?

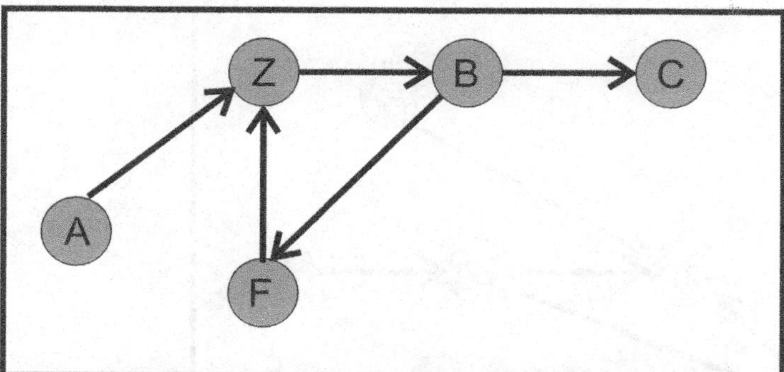

Solution:

ZBFZ

23. Does this graph has cyclic closed path?

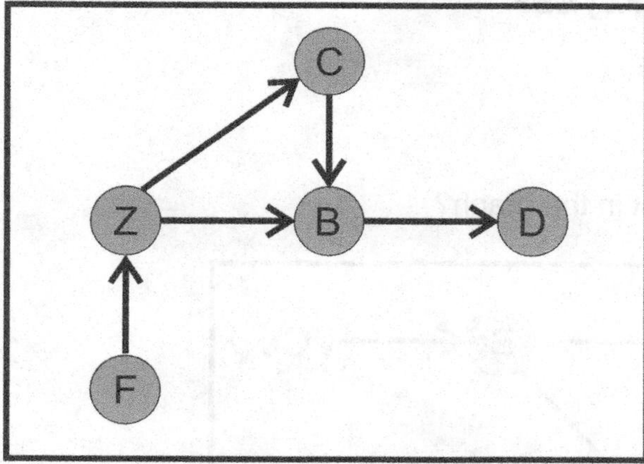

Solution:

No

24. How many paths of length 2 exist in the graph?

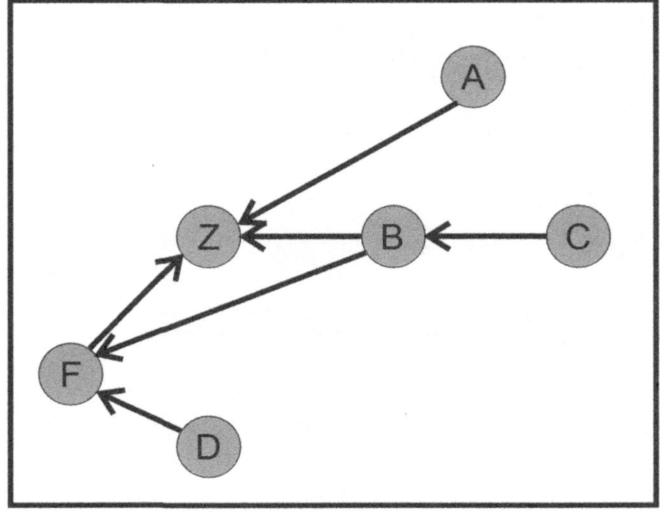

Solution:

4

CBZ , DFZ , BFZ , CBF

25. How many paths of length 2 exist in the graph?

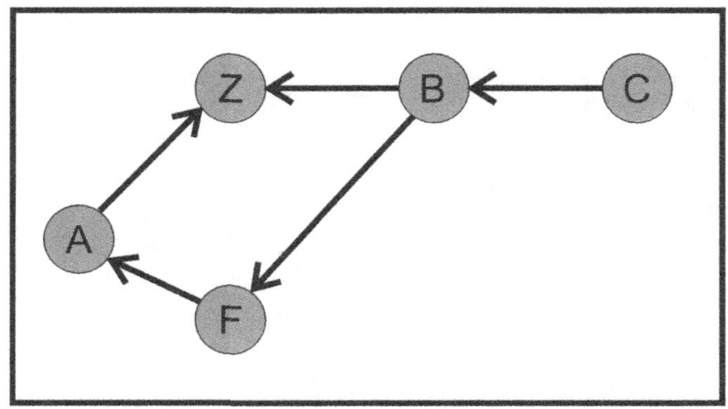

Solution:

3

CBF , FAZ , BFA

26. What is the adjacency matrix of the graph?

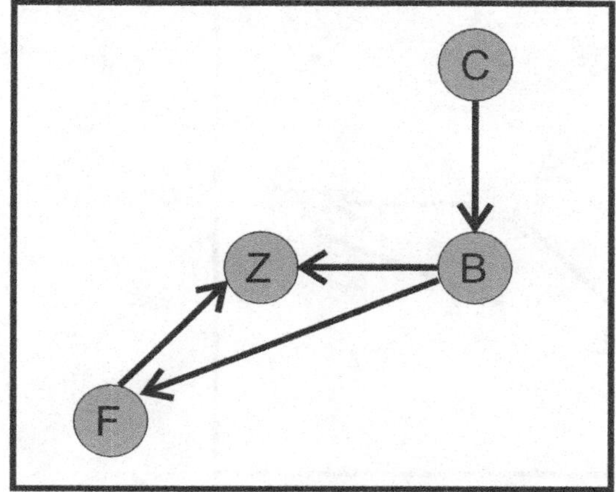

Solution:

	B	C	F	Z
B	0	0	1	1
C	1	0	0	0
F	0	0	0	1
Z	0	0	0	0

27. Does this graph have a cycle?

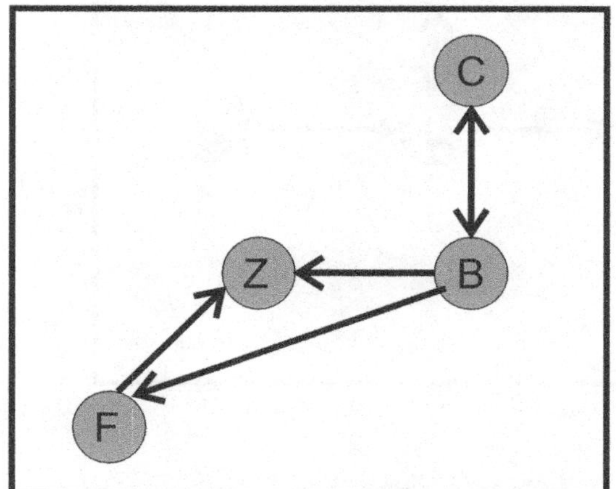

Solution:

CBC

28. How many paths of length 2 exist in graph?

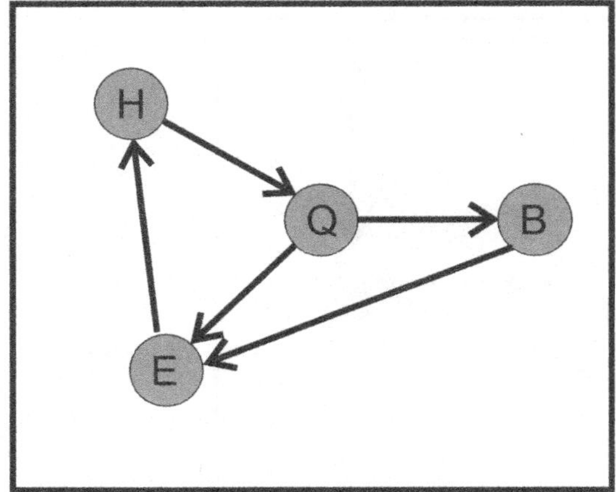

Solution:

6

HQB , QBE , QEH , HQE , BEH , EHQ

29. What are the cycles in the graph?

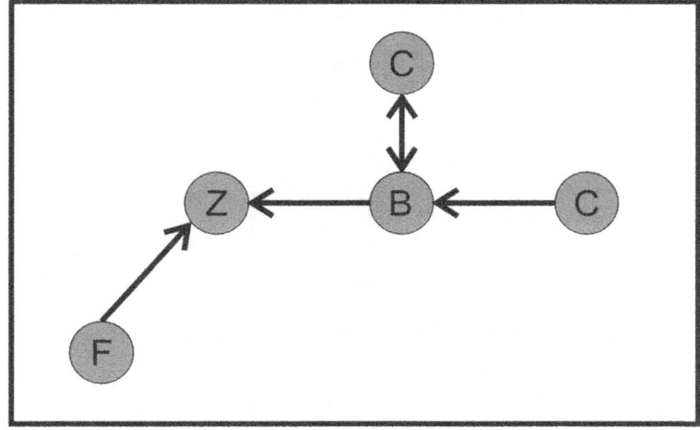

Solution:

BCB

30. How many paths of length 2 exist in the graph?

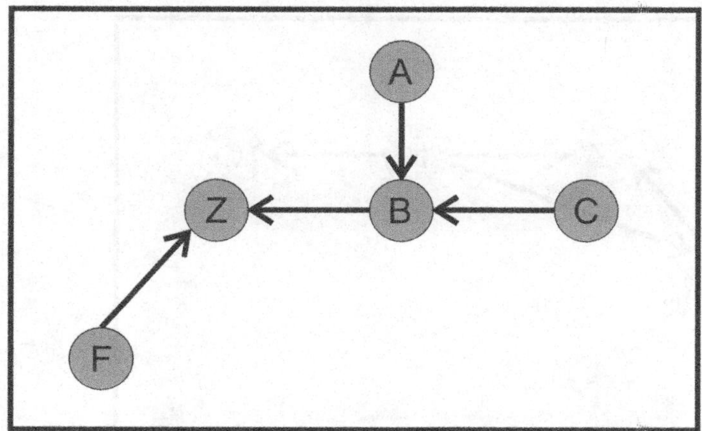

Solution:

2

CBZ,ABZ

31. How many paths of length 2 exist in the graph?

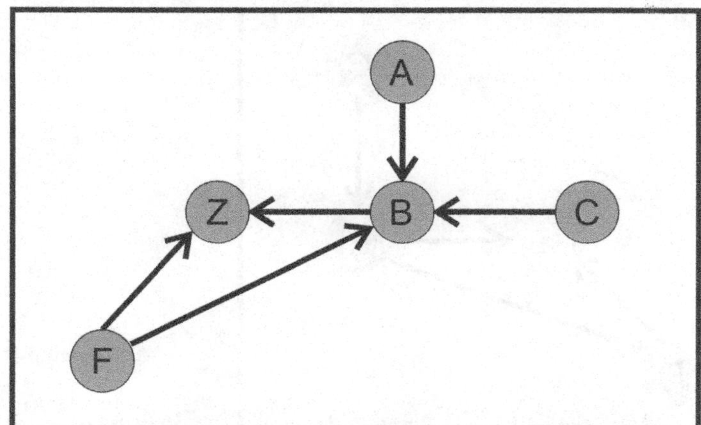

Solution:

2

CBZ,ABZ

32. What node is directing towards two or more node?

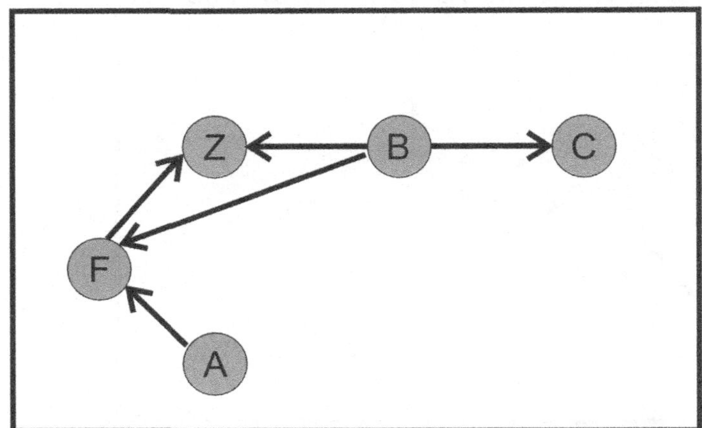

Solution:

Node B

33. How many paths of length 2 exist in graph?

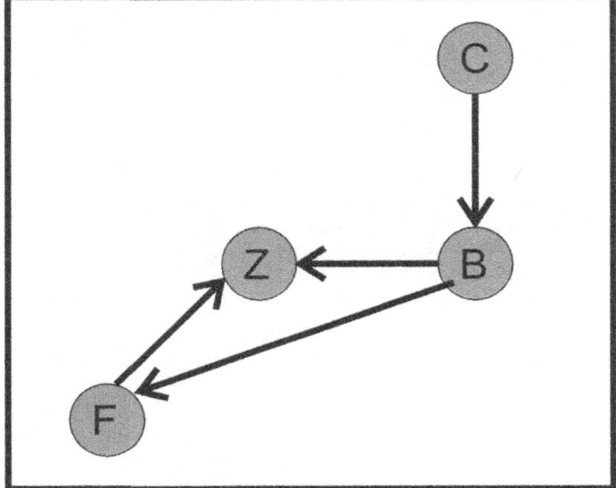

Solution:

3
CBZ,BFZ,CBF

34. Draw the graph:

	B	E	H	Q
B	0	1	0	0
E	0	0	1	0
H	0	0	0	1
Q	1	1	0	0

Solution:

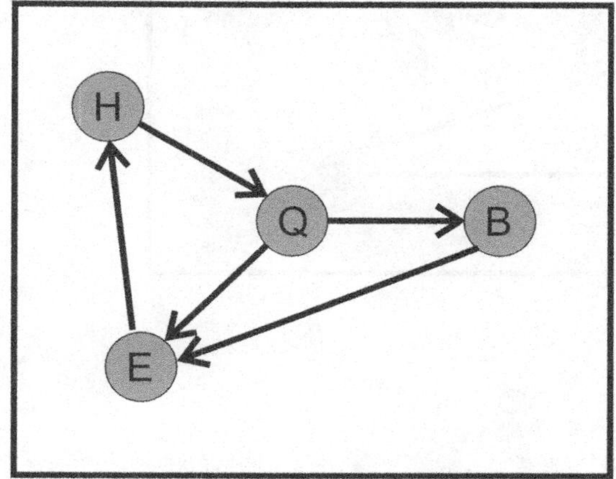

35. What are the cycles in the graph?

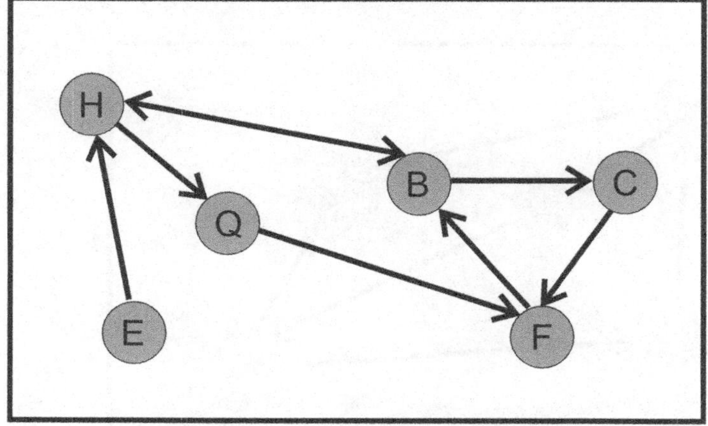

Solution:

HBH, HQFB H, BCFB

36. What are the cycles in the graph?

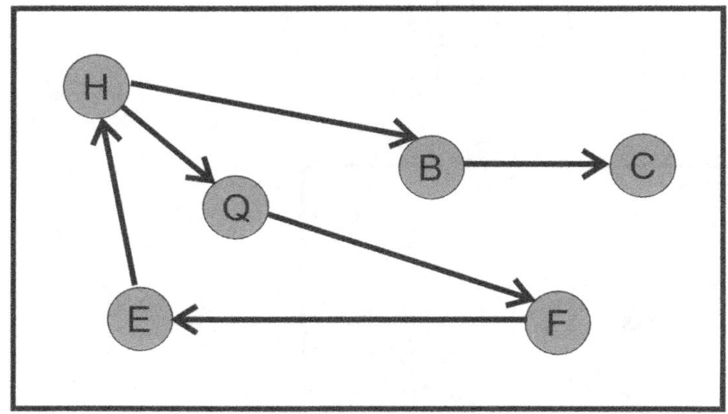

Solution:

HQFEH, HBH

37. What are cycles in the graph?

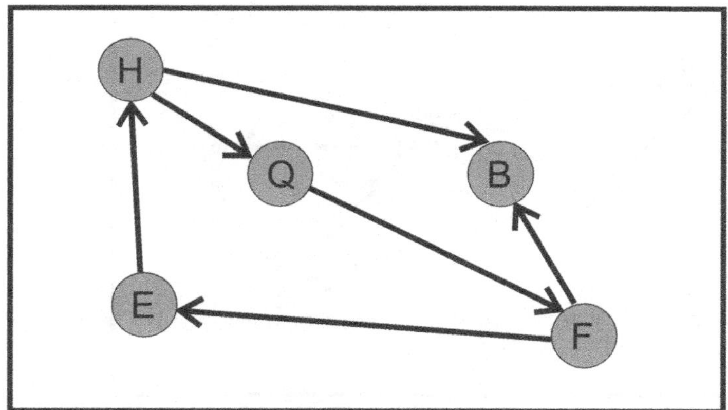

Solution:

HQFEH, HBH, HQFBH

38. Is there a closed cyclic path in the graph?

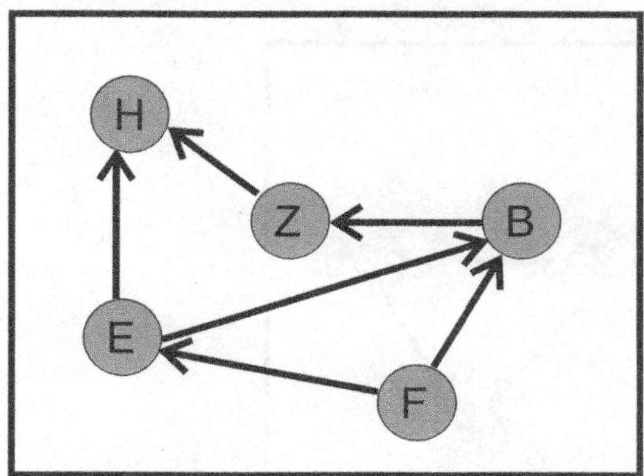

Solution:

No

39. What is the adjacency matrix of the graph?

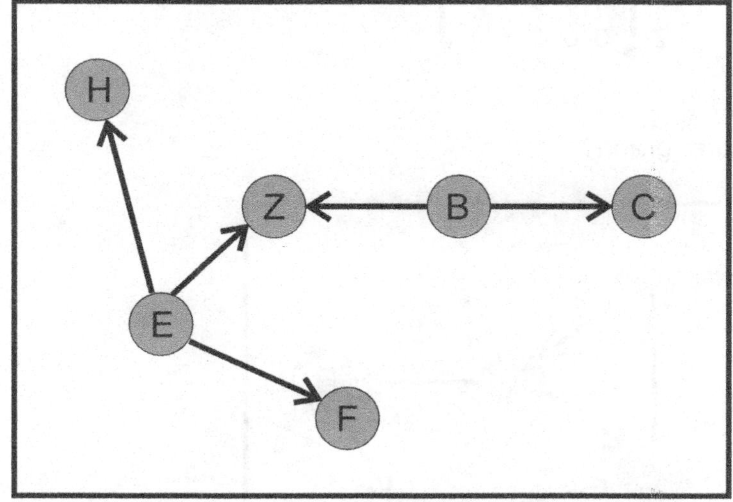

Solution:

	B	C	E	F	H	Z
B	0	1	0	0	0	1
C	0	0	0	0	0	0
E	0	1	0	1	1	0
F	0	0	0	0	0	0
H	0	0	0	0	0	0
Z	0	0	0	0	0	0

40. What is the adjacency matrix for the graph?

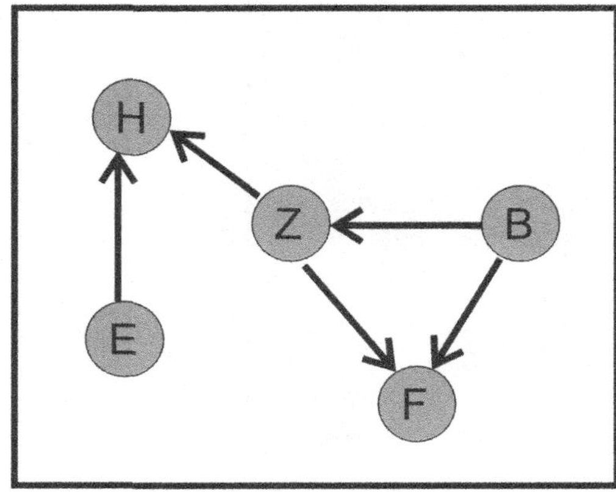

Solution:

	B	E	F	H	Z
B	0	0	1	0	1
E	0	0	0	1	0
F	0	0	0	0	0
H	0	0	0	0	0
Z	0	0	1	1	0

41. What are the cycles in the graph?

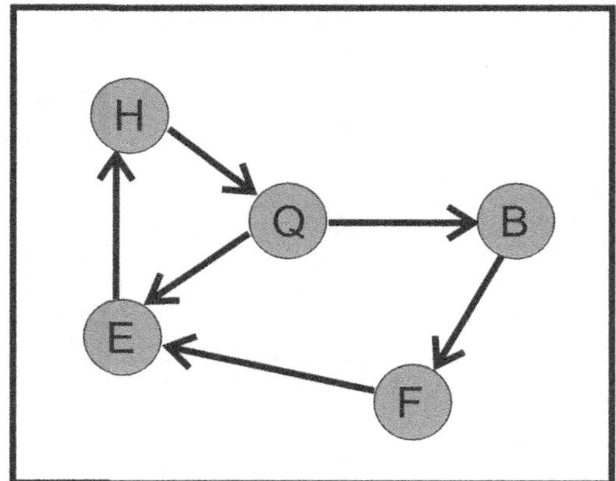

Solution:

HQBFEH, HQEH

42. What are the cycles in the graph?

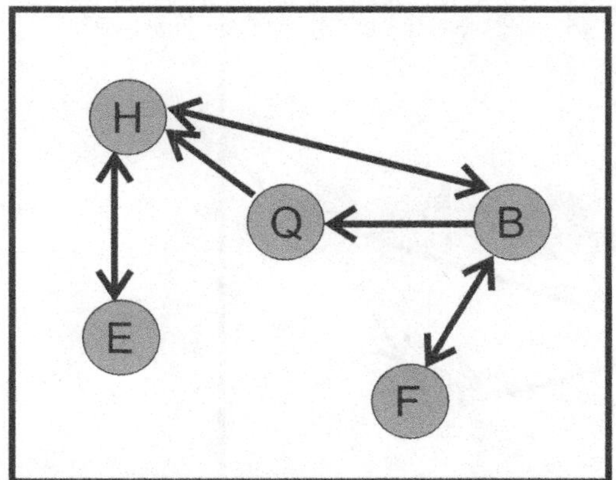

Solution:

HBH, HEH, BFB, BQHB

43. What is adjacency matrix of the graph?

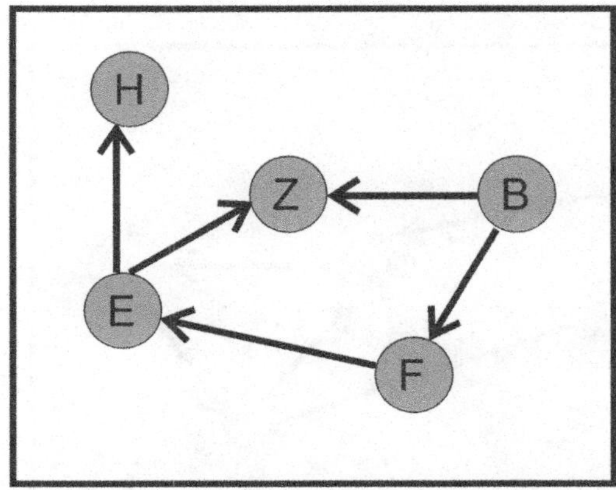

Solution:

$$\begin{array}{c} \\ B \\ E \\ F \\ H \\ Z \end{array} \begin{array}{c} \begin{array}{ccccc} B & E & F & H & Z \end{array} \\ \begin{bmatrix} 0 & 0 & 1 & 0 & 1 \\ 0 & 0 & 0 & 0 & 1 \\ 0 & 1 & 0 & 0 & 0 \\ 0 & 0 & 0 & 0 & 0 \\ 0 & 0 & 0 & 0 & 0 \end{bmatrix} \end{array}$$

44. What are the cycles in the graph?

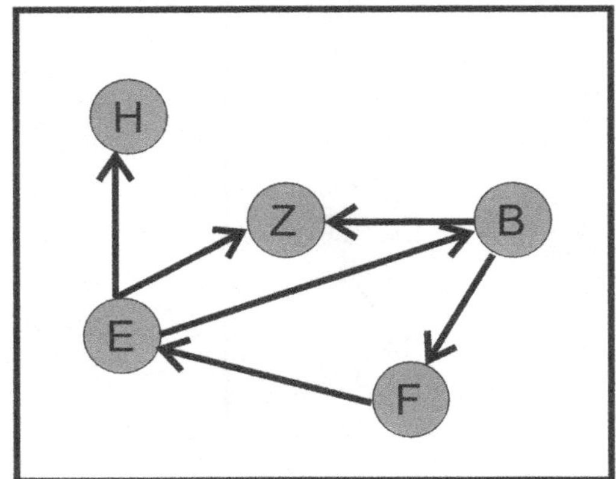

Solution:

EBFE

45. What are the cycles in the graph?

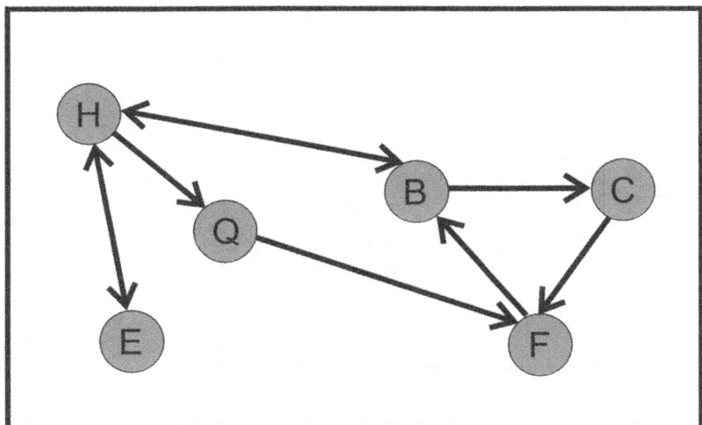

Solution:

BCFB, HBH, HEH

46. How many paths of length 2 are in the graph?

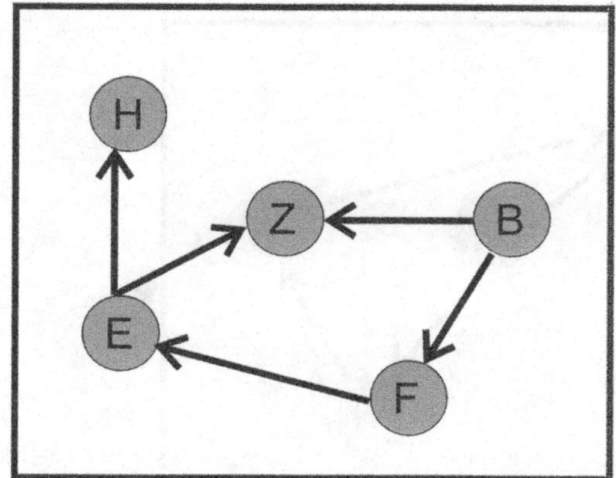

Solution:

2

BFE,FEZ

47. What are the cycles in the graph?

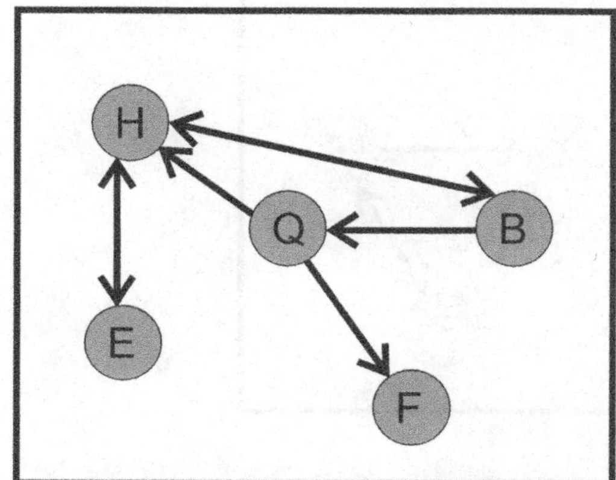

Solution:

HBQH, HEH, HBH

48. What are the cycles of the graph?

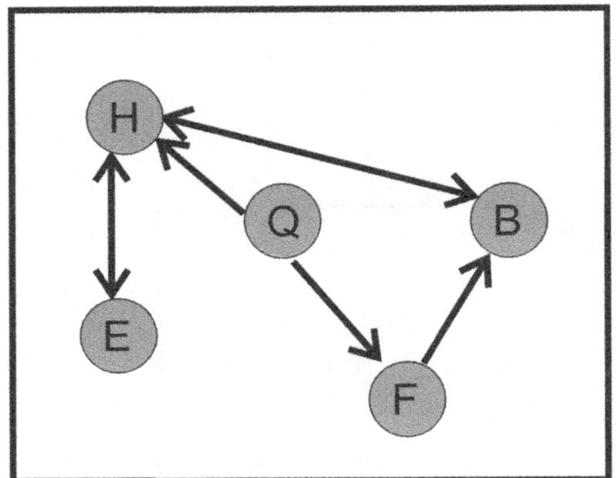

Solution:

HBH, HEH

49. What are the cycles in the graph?

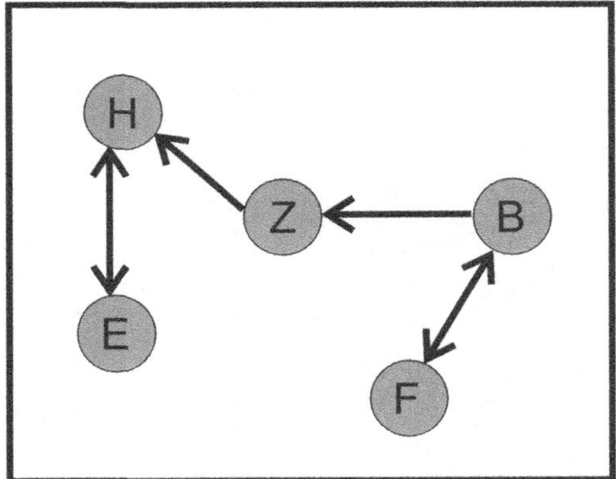

Solution:

HEH, BFB

50. How many paths of length 2 exist in the graph?

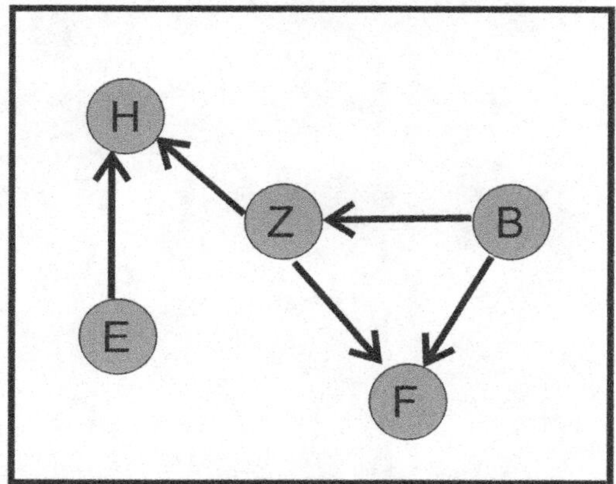

Solution:

1

MK
MATH
KNOTS
Joy of Learning....

1. Simplify the following Logic gate using truth table.

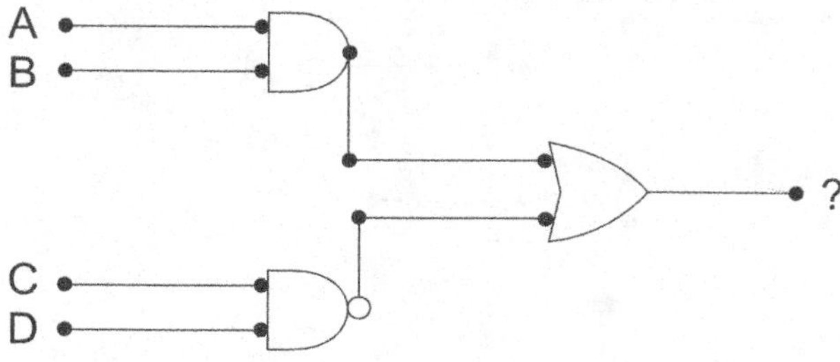

Solution:

$= (A.B) + (\overline{C} + \overline{D})$

A	B	C	D	A.B	NOT(C.D	A.B OR NOT(C.D
0	0	0	0	0	1	1
0	0	0	1	0	1	1
0	0	1	0	0	1	1
0	0	1	1	0	0	0
0	1	0	0	0	1	1
0	1	0	1	0	1	1
0	1	1	0	0	1	1
0	1	1	1	0	0	0
1	0	0	0	1	1	1
1	0	0	1	1	1	1
1	0	1	0	1	1	1
1	0	1	1	0	0	0
1	1	0	0	1	1	1
1	1	0	1	1	1	1
1	1	1	0	1	1	1
1	1	1	1	1	0	1

2. Translate into Boolean expression.

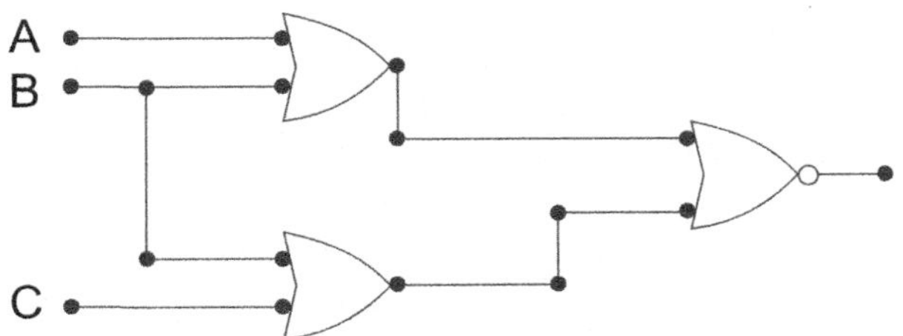

Solution:

$$\overline{(A + B) + (B + C)}$$

3. Simplify the following Logic gate using truth table.

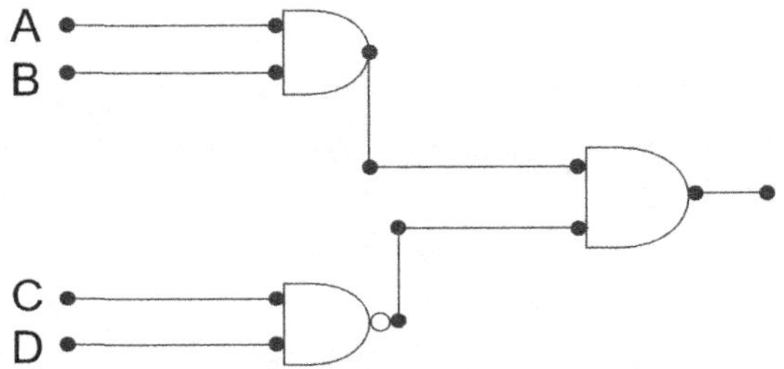

Solution:

$$(A.B).(\overline{C}+ \overline{D}) = A.B.\overline{C} + A.B.\overline{D}$$

A	B	C	D	A.B	$(\overline{C} + \overline{D})$	A.B AND $(\overline{C} + D)$
0	0	0	0	0	1	1
0	0	0	1	0	1	1
0	0	1	0	0	1	1
0	0	1	1	0	0	0
0	1	0	0	0	1	1
0	1	0	1	0	1	1
0	1	1	0	0	1	1
0	1	1	1	0	0	0
1	0	0	0	0	1	1
1	0	0	1	0	1	1
1	0	1	0	0	1	1
1	0	1	1	0	0	0
1	1	0	0	1	1	1
1	1	0	1	1	1	1
1	1	1	0	1	1	1
1	1	1	1	1	0	1

4. Simplify the following Logic gate using the truth table.

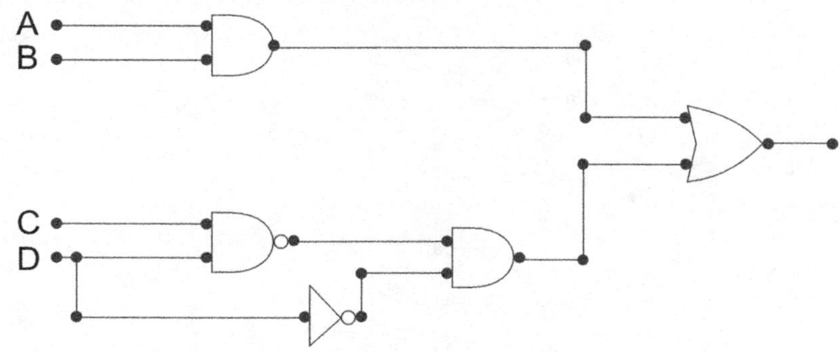

Solution:

$A.B + \bar{C}.\bar{D} + \bar{D}$

A	B	C	D	A.B	$\bar{C}.\bar{D}$	$\bar{C} + \bar{D}$	(A.B) + $\bar{C} + \bar{D}$
0	0	0	0	0	1	1	1
0	0	0	1	0	1	0	1
0	0	1	0	0	1	1	1
0	0	1	1	0	0	0	0
0	1	0	0	0	1	1	1
0	1	0	1	0	1	0	1
0	1	1	0	0	1	1	1
0	1	1	1	0	0	0	0
1	0	0	0	0	1	1	1
1	0	0	1	0	1	0	1
1	0	1	0	0	1	1	1
1	0	1	1	0	0	0	0
1	1	0	0	1	1	1	1
1	1	0	1	1	1	0	1
1	1	1	0	1	1	1	1
1	1	1	1	1	0	0	0

5. Translate into Boolean expression.

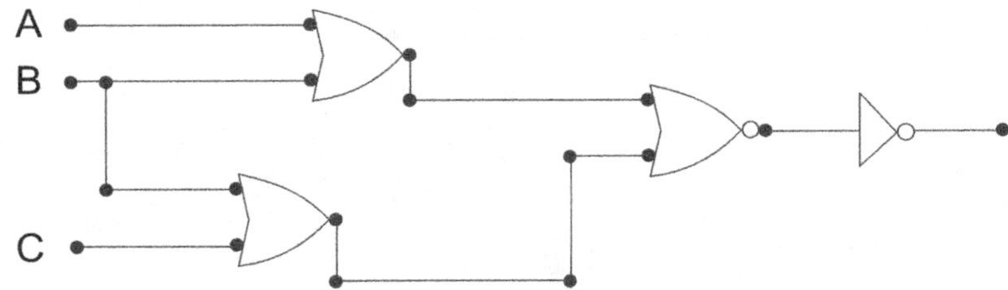

Solution:

$$\overline{\overline{(A + B) + (B + C)}} = (A + B) + (B + C)$$

6. Simplify using truth table.

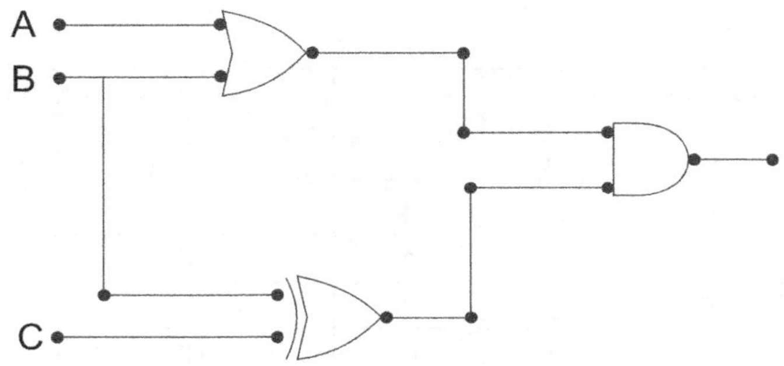

Solution:

$(A+B).(B \oplus C)$

A	B	C	A OR B	B XOR C	(A OR B) AND (B XOR C)
0	0	0	0	0	0
0	0	1	0	1	0
0	1	0	1	1	1
0	1	1	1	0	0
1	0	0	1	0	0
1	0	1	1	1	1
1	1	0	1	1	1
1	1	1	1	0	0

7. Simplify the Logic gate using truth table.

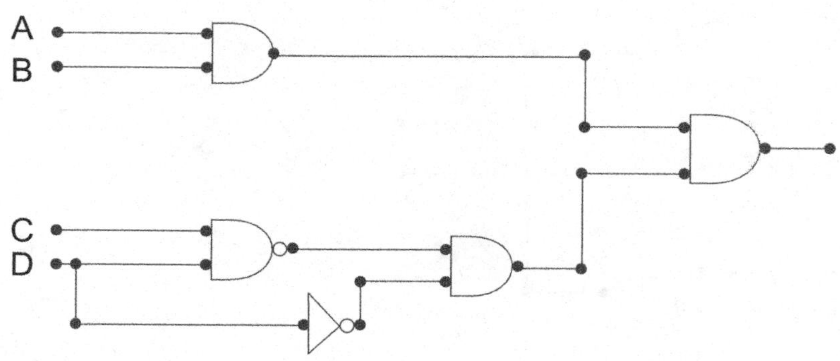

Solution:

$A.B.\overline{D}\ (\overline{C} + \overline{D})$

A	B	C	D	A.B	$(\overline{C} + \overline{D})$	$\overline{D}\ (\overline{C} + \overline{D})$	$AB\overline{D}\ (\overline{C} + \overline{D})$
0	0	0	0	0	1	1	0
0	0	0	1	0	1	0	0
0	0	1	0	0	1	1	0
0	0	1	1	0	0	0	0
0	1	0	0	0	1	1	0
0	1	0	1	0	1	0	0
0	1	1	0	0	1	1	0
0	1	1	1	0	0	0	0
1	0	0	0	0	0	0	0
1	0	0	1	0	0	0	0
1	0	1	0	0	0	0	0
1	0	1	1	0	0	0	0
1	1	0	0	1	0	0	0
1	1	0	1	1	0	0	0
1	1	1	0	1	0	0	0
1	1	1	1	1	0	0	0

8. Simplify using truth table.

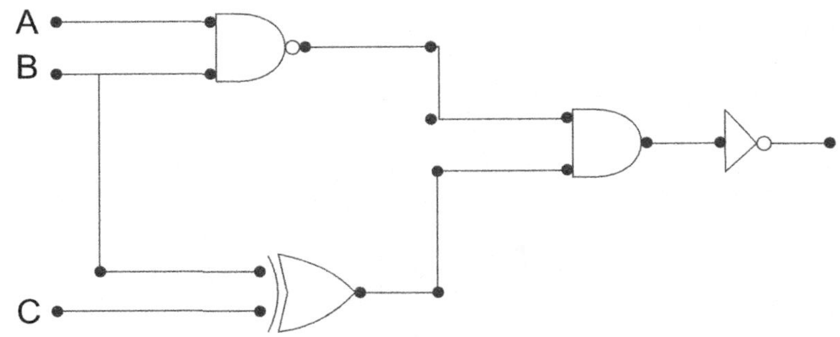

Solution:

$$\overline{\overline{A.B}.(C \oplus D)} = A.B + \overline{(C \oplus D)}$$

A	B	C	D	(A.B)	NOT(XOR(C.D))	(A.B)+ NOT(XOR(C.D))
0	0	0	0	0	1	0
0	0	0	1	0	0	0
0	0	1	0	0	0	0
0	0	1	1	0	1	0
0	1	0	0	0	1	0
0	1	0	1	0	0	0
0	1	1	0	0	0	0
0	1	1	1	0	1	0
1	0	0	0	0	1	0
1	0	0	1	0	0	0
1	0	1	0	0	0	0
1	0	1	1	0	1	0
1	1	0	0	1	1	1
1	1	0	1	1	0	0
1	1	1	0	1	0	0
1	1	1	1	1	1	1

9. Translate into Boolean expression

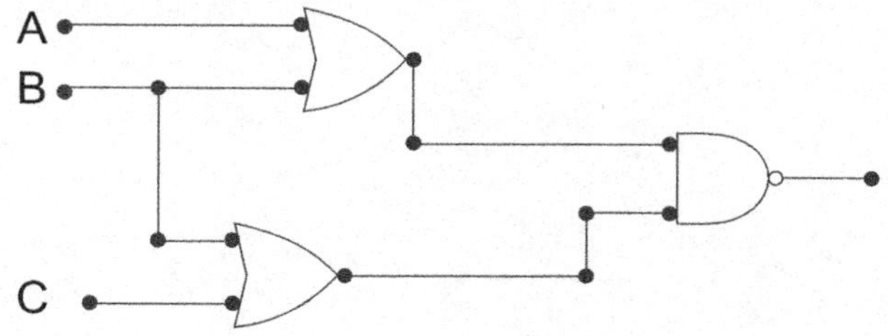

Solution:

$$\overline{(A + B).(C + B)} = \overline{(A + B)} + \overline{(C + B)} = \bar{A}.\bar{B} + \bar{C}.\bar{B}$$

10. Translate into Boolean expression.

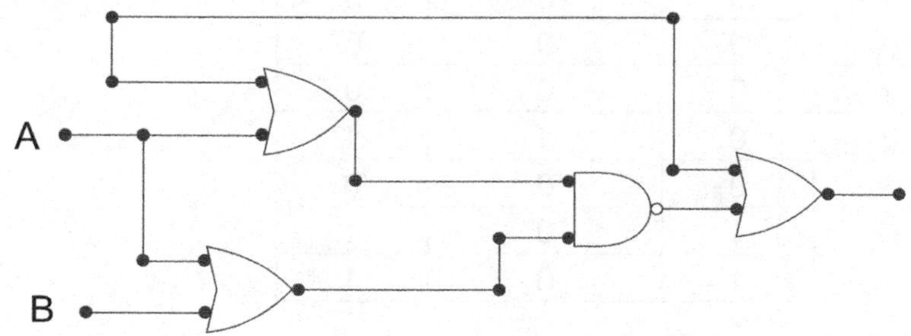

Solution

$$A + \overline{(A + B).(B + C)} = \bar{A}.\bar{B} + \bar{B}.\bar{C} + A$$

11. Translate into Boolean expression.

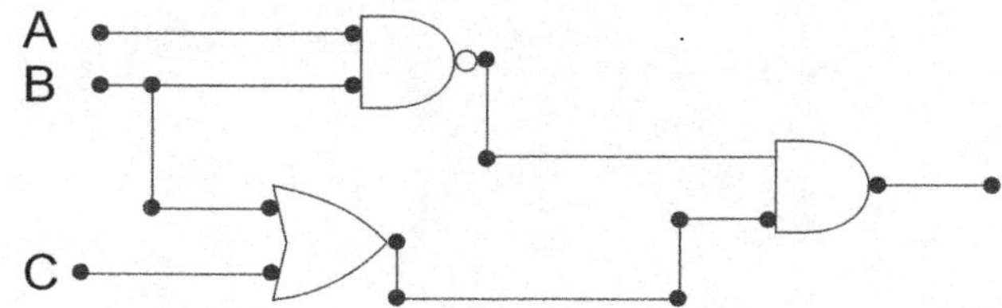

Solution:

$$(\overline{A.B}).(B + C) = (\bar{A} + \bar{B}).(B + C)$$

12. Mention the triplets for which the result is TRUE.

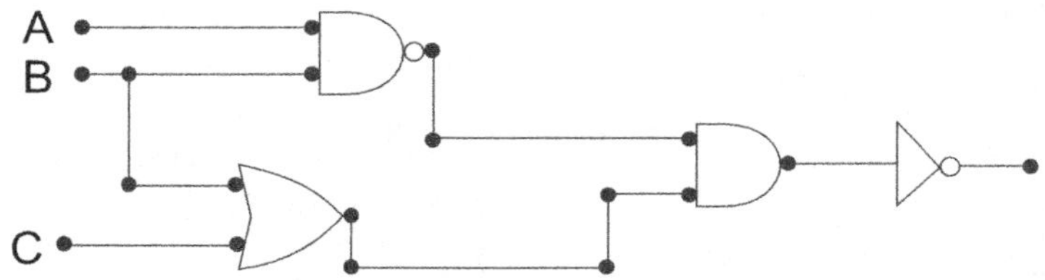

Solution:

(000,100, 110, 111)

A	B	C	A AND B	$\overline{B}.\overline{C}$	A.B + $\overline{B}.\overline{C}$
0	0	0	0	1	1
0	0	1	0	0	0
0	1	0	0	0	0
0	1	1	0	0	0
1	0	0	0	1	1
1	0	1	0	0	0
1	1	0	1	0	1
1	1	1	1	0	1

13. Translate into Boolean expression.

A
B
C

Solution:

$(\overline{A} + \overline{B}) + \overline{C}$

14. Translate into Boolean expression.

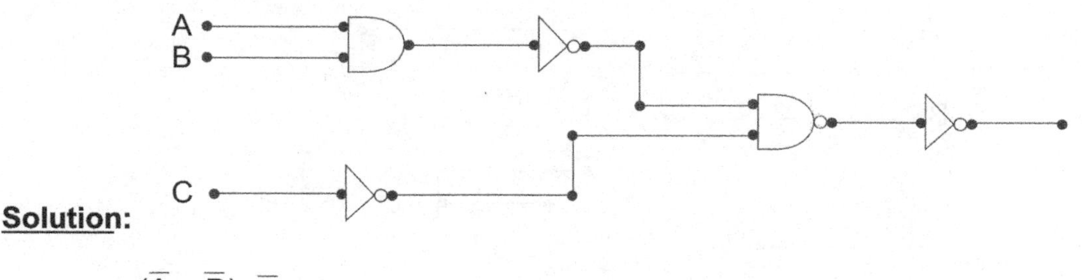

Solution:

$(\overline{A} + \overline{B}).\ \overline{C}$

15. Simply using truth table.

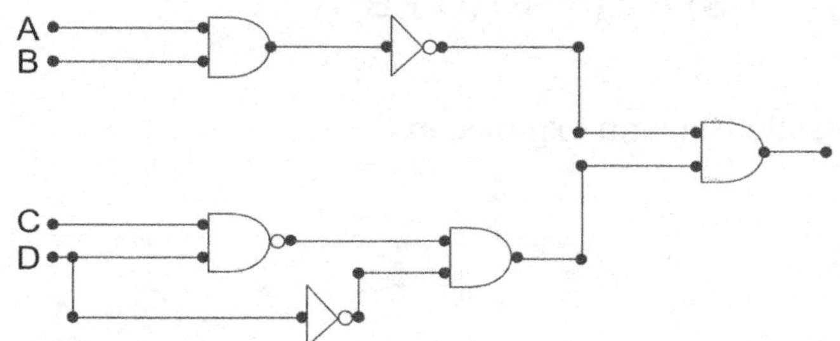

Solution:

$(\overline{A} + \overline{B}).(\overline{C}.\overline{D} + \overline{D})$

A	B	C	D	$(\overline{A} + \overline{B})$	NOT(C.D)	NOT(D) AND NOT(C.D) =	NOT(A.B) AND NOT(D) AND NOT(C.D) =
0	0	0	0	1	1	1	1
0	0	0	1	1	1	0	0
0	0	1	0	1	1	1	1
0	0	1	1	1	0	0	0
0	1	0	0	1	1	1	1
0	1	0	1	1	1	1	0
0	1	1	0	1	1	1	1
0	1	1	1	1	0	0	0
1	0	0	0	1	1	1	1
1	0	0	1	1	1	0	0
1	0	1	0	1	1	1	1
1	0	1	1	1	0	0	0
1	1	0	0	0	1	1	0
1	1	0	1	0	1	0	0
1	1	1	0	0	1	1	0
1	1	1	1	0	0	0	0

16. Translate into Boolean expression.

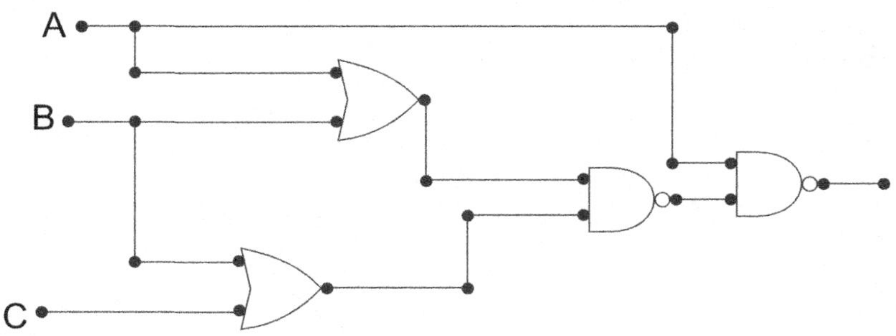

Solution:

$$\overline{\overline{(A + B).(C + B)}.\overline{A}} = (A + B).(C + B).\overline{A}$$

17. Translate the following into Boolean expression.

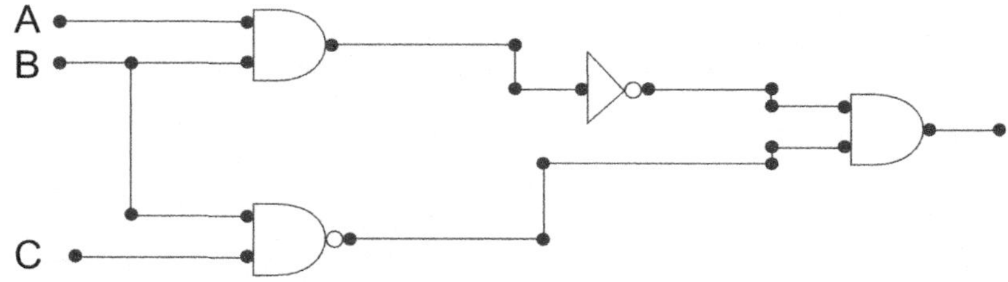

Solution:

$$(\overline{A} + \overline{B}).(\overline{B} + \overline{C})$$

18. Translate the following Boolean Expression.

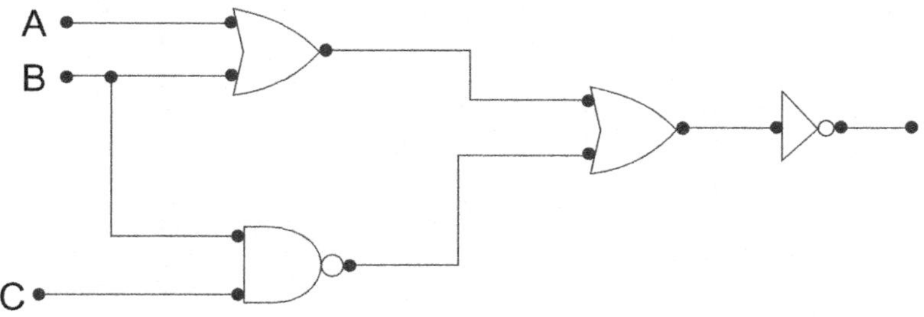

Solution:

$$\overline{(A + B) + \overline{B.C}} = (\overline{A}.\overline{B}).(B.C)$$

19. Find the triplet for which the solution is TRUE

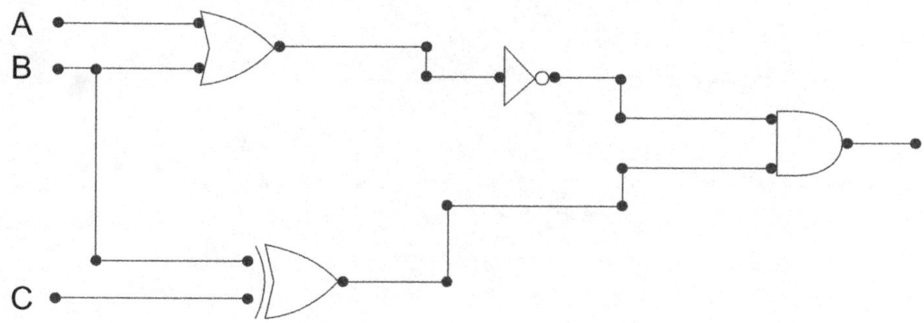

Solution:

$\overline{(A + B)}.(B \oplus C)$

(001)

A	B	C	NOT(A OR B)	B XOR C	NOT(A OR B) AND(B XOR C)
0	0	0	1	0	0
0	0	1	1	1	1
0	1	0	0	1	0
0	1	1	0	0	0
1	0	0	0	0	0
1	0	1	0	1	0
1	1	0	0	1	0
1	1	1	0	0	0

20. Translate the following to Boolean expression.

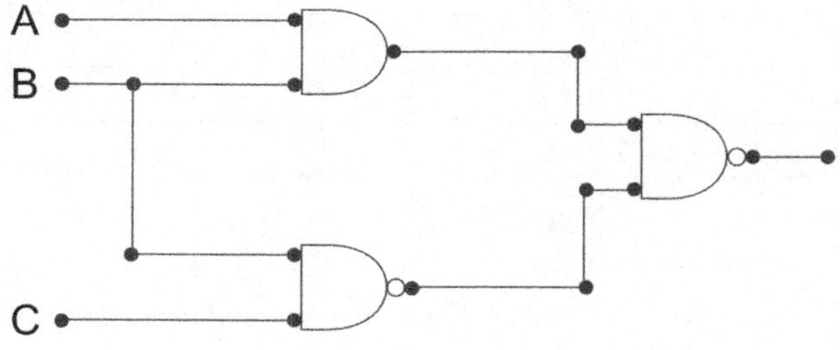

Solution:

$(\bar{A} + \bar{B}) + B.C$

21. Simplify using truth table.

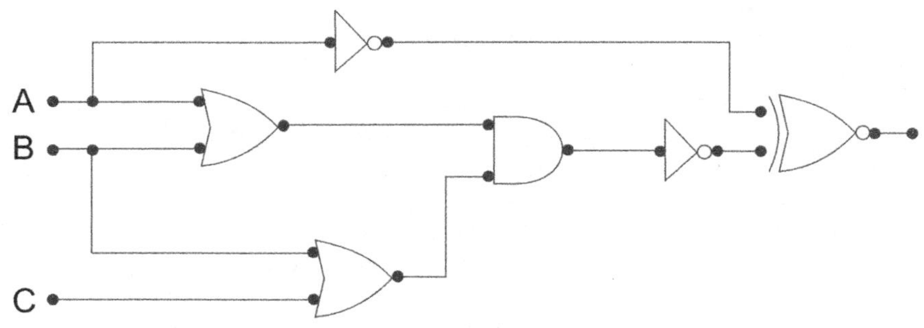

Solution:

$\overline{A} \oplus (A + B).(B + C)$

A	B	C	A OR B	B OR C	(A OR B) AND (B OR C	NOT((A OR B) AND (B OR C))	NOT A XNOR (NOT((A OR B) AND (B OR C)))
0	0	0	0	0	0	1	0
0	0	1	0	1	0	1	0
0	1	0	1	1	1	0	1
0	1	1	1	1	1	0	1
1	0	0	1	0	0	1	1
1	0	1	1	1	1	0	0
1	1	0	1	1	1	0	0
1	1	1	1	1	1	0	0

22. Simplify usingtruth table.

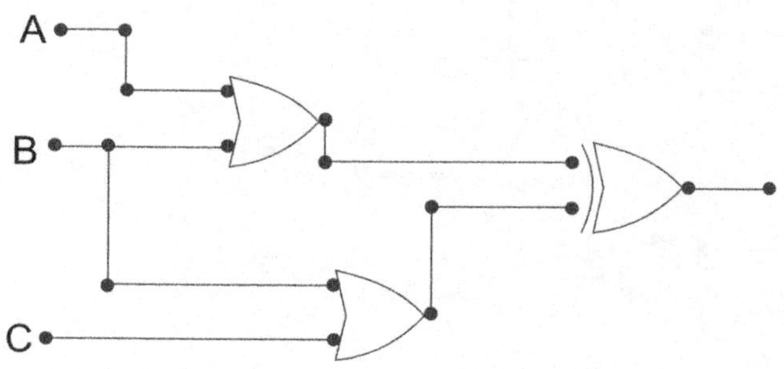

Solution:

(A + B) ⊕ (B + C)

A	B	C	A OR B	B OR C	(A OR B) XOR (B OR C
0	0	0	0	0	0
0	0	1	0	1	1
0	1	0	1	1	0
0	1	1	1	1	0
1	0	0	1	0	1
1	0	1	1	1	0
1	1	0	1	1	0
1	1	1	1	1	0

23. Translate the following to Boolean expression.

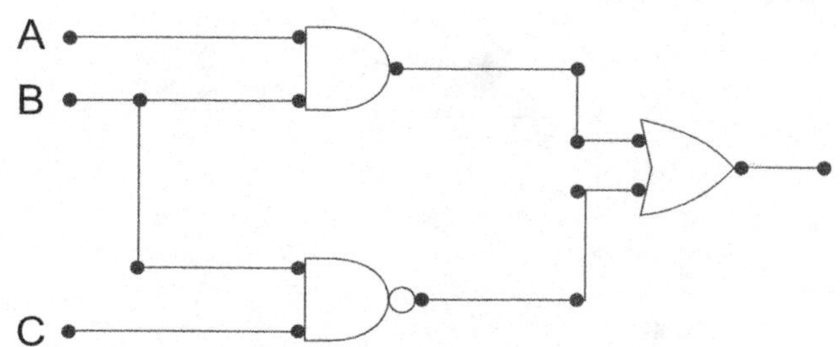

Solution:

$\overline{(A.B) + \overline{(B.C)}}$

24. For which triplets is the solution FALSE

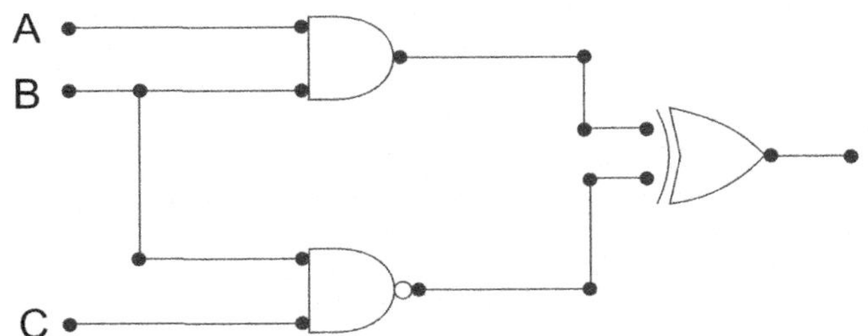

Solution:

(111 , 101 , 100 , 000 , 001 , 010)

A	B	C	A AND B	NOT(B AND C)	(A AND B) XOR NOT(B AND C)
0	0	0	0	1	1
0	0	1	0	1	1
0	1	0	0	1	1
0	1	1	0	0	0
1	0	0	0	1	1
1	0	1	0	1	1
1	1	0	1	1	0
1	1	1	1	0	1

25. Translate into Boolean expression.

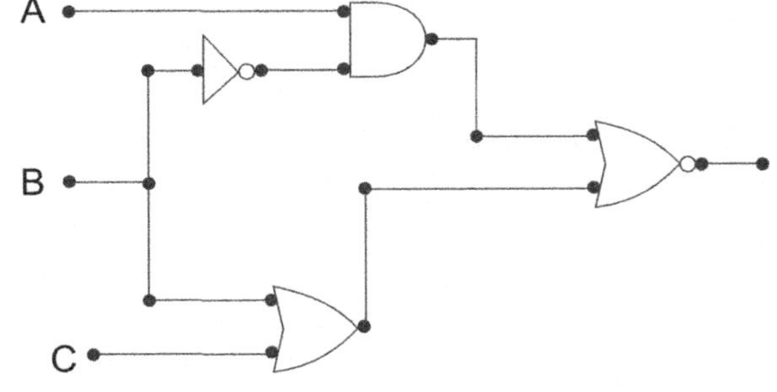

Solution:

$(\overline{A} + B).(\overline{B}.\overline{C})$

26. Simplify using truth table.

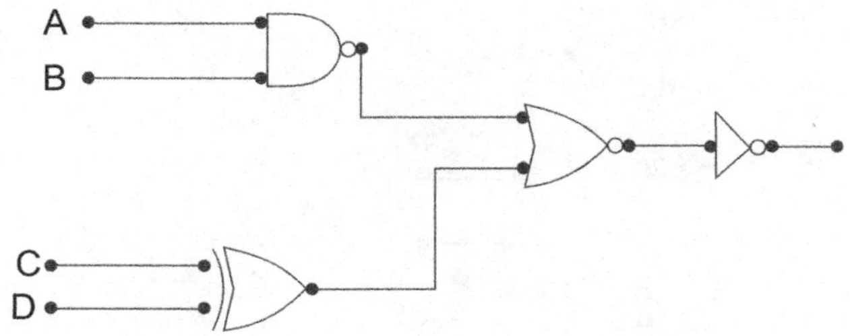

Solution:

$(\overline{A} + \overline{B}) + (C \oplus D)$

A	B	C	D	NOT(A.B)	XOR(C.D)	NOT(A.B)NOR XOR(C.D)	NOT(NOT(A.B)NOR(C.D))
0	0	0	0	1	0	0	1
0	0	0	1	1	1	0	1
0	0	1	0	1	1	0	1
0	0	1	1	1	0	0	1
0	1	0	0	1	0	0	1
0	1	0	1	1	1	0	1
0	1	1	0	1	1	0	1
0	1	1	1	1	0	0	1
1	0	0	0	1	0	0	1
1	0	0	1	1	1	0	0
1	0	1	0	1	1	0	1
1	0	1	1	1	0	0	1
1	1	0	0	0	0	1	0
1	1	0	1	0	1	0	1
1	1	1	0	0	1	0	1
1	1	1	1	0	0	1	0

27. Translate into Boolean expression.

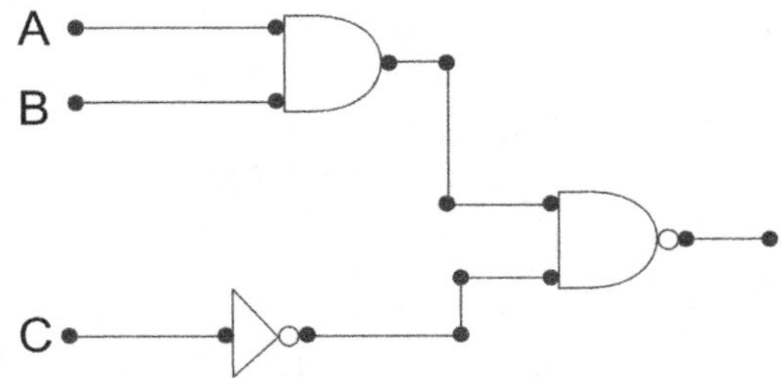

Solution:

$(\overline{A} + \overline{B}) + C$

28. Translate using Boolean expression.

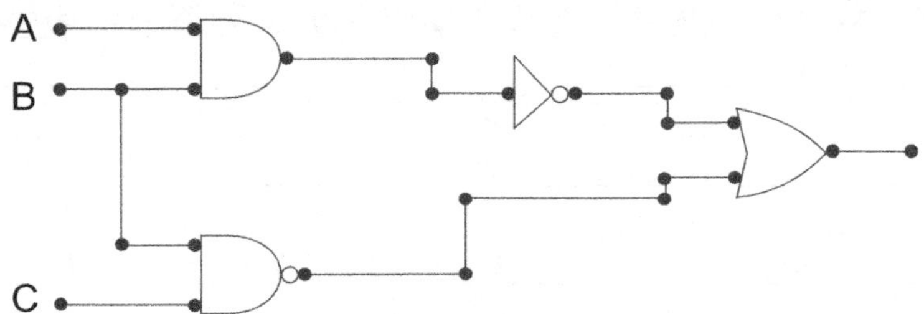

Solution:

$(\overline{A} + \overline{B}) + (\overline{B} + \overline{C})$

29. Translate into Boolean expression.

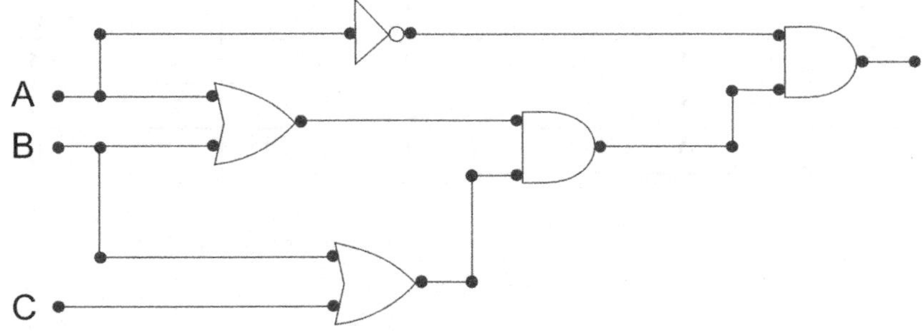

Solution:

$\overline{A}.((A + B).(B + C))$

30. Simplify using truth table.

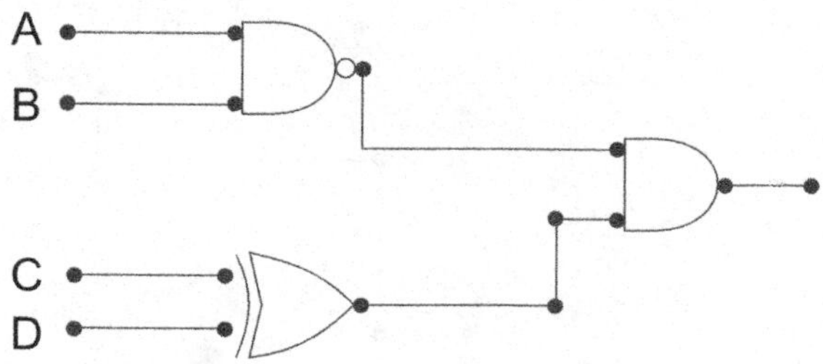

Solution:

$(\overline{A} + \overline{B}).(C \oplus D)$

A	B	C	D	NOT(A.B)	XOR(C.D)	NOT(A.B) AND XOR(C.D)
0	0	0	0	1	0	0
0	0	0	1	1	1	1
0	0	1	0	1	1	1
0	0	1	1	1	0	0
0	1	0	0	1	0	0
0	1	0	1	1	1	1
0	1	1	0	1	1	1
0	1	1	1	1	0	0
1	0	0	0	1	0	0
1	0	0	1	1	1	1
1	0	1	0	1	1	1
1	0	1	1	1	0	0
1	1	0	0	0	0	0
1	1	0	1	0	1	0
1	1	1	0	0	1	0
1	1	1	1	0	0	0

31. Translate the following into Boolean.

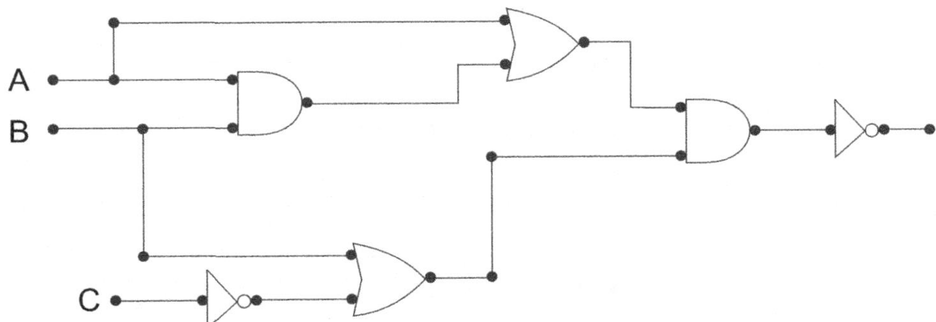

Solution:

$\overline{((A.B) + A).(B + \overline{C})}$

32. Simplify using truth table. For which triplets is the solution TRUE

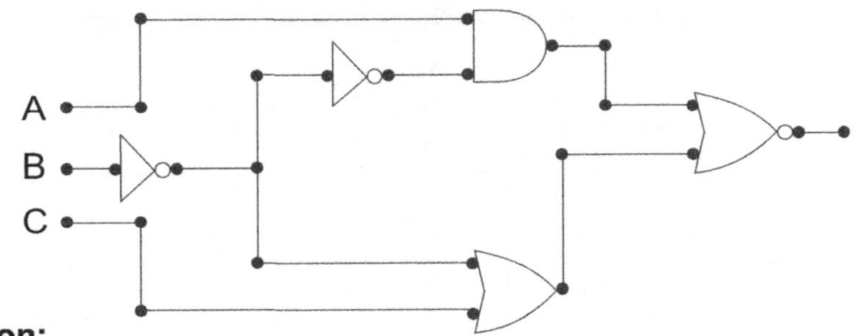

Solution:

$(\overline{A} + \overline{B}).(B.\overline{C})$

(010)

A	B	C	A AND B	C OR NOT B	(A AND B) NOR (C OR NOT B)
0	0	0	0	1	0
0	0	1	0	1	0
0	1	0	0	0	1
0	1	1	0	1	0
1	0	0	0	1	0
1	0	1	0	1	0
1	1	0	1	0	0
1	1	1	1	1	0

33. Translate the expression.

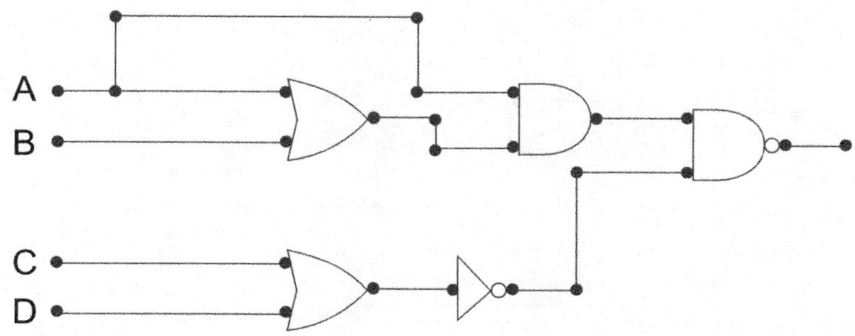

Solution:

$$\overline{(A.(A + B)).\overline{(C + B)}}$$

34. Translate into Boolean expression.

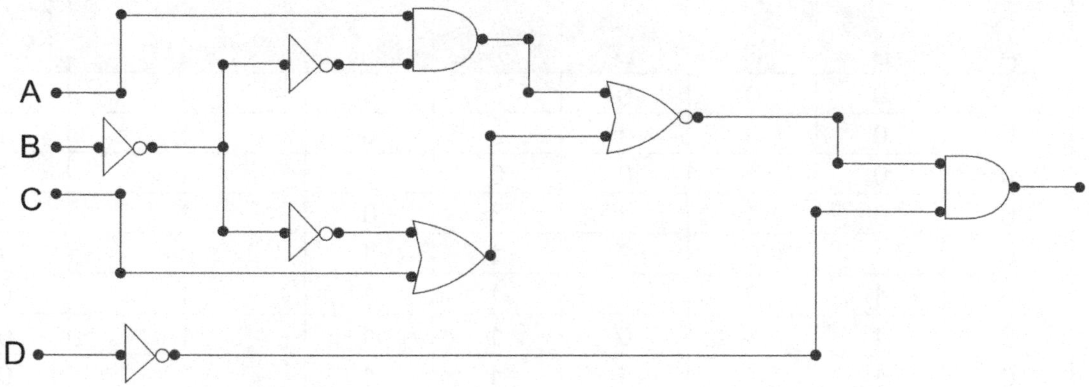

Solution:

$$(\overline{D}.\overline{A} + \overline{D}.\overline{B}).(\overline{D}.\overline{B}.\overline{C})$$

35. Simplify the expression using truth table.

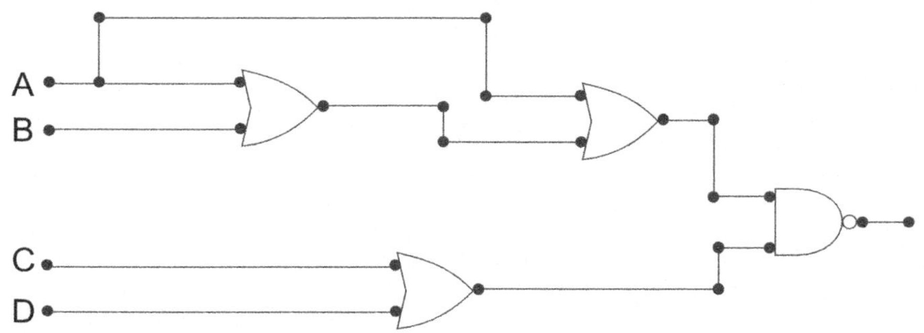

Solution:

$(\bar{A}.(\bar{A}.\bar{B})) + (\bar{C}.\bar{D})$

A	B	C	D	A OR B	A OR (A OR B)	C OR D	A OR (A OR B) NAND (C OR D)
0	0	0	0	0	0	0	1
0	0	0	1	0	0	1	1
0	0	1	0	0	0	1	1
0	0	1	1	0	0	1	1
0	1	0	0	1	1	0	1
0	1	0	1	1	1	1	0
0	1	1	0	1	1	1	0
0	1	1	1	1	1	1	0
1	0	0	0	1	1	0	1
1	0	0	1	1	1	1	0
1	0	1	0	1	1	1	0
1	0	1	1	1	1	1	0
1	1	0	0	1	1	0	1
1	1	0	1	1	1	1	0
1	1	1	0	1	1	1	0
1	1	1	1	1	1	1	0

36. Translate the following into Boolean expression.

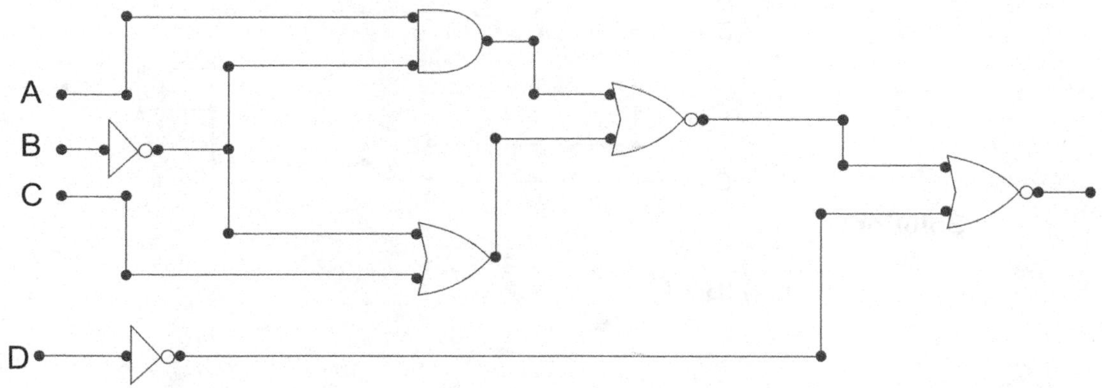

Solution:

$\overline{A.\overline{B} + (\overline{B} + C)} + \overline{D}$

37. Simplify using truth table. For which triplets is the solution TRUE.

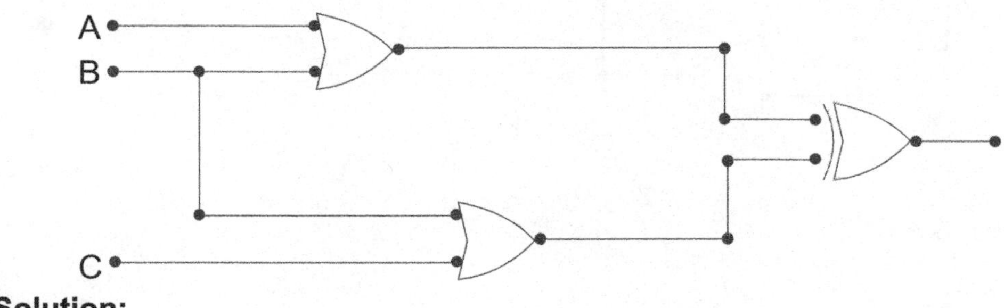

Solution:

$(A + B) \oplus (B + C)$

(001, 100)

A	B	C	A OR B	B OR C	(A OR B) XOR (B OR C
0	0	0	0	0	0
0	0	1	0	1	1
0	1	0	1	1	0
0	1	1	1	1	0
1	0	0	1	0	1
1	0	1	1	1	0
1	1	0	1	1	0
1	1	1	1	1	0

38. Translate into Boolean expression.

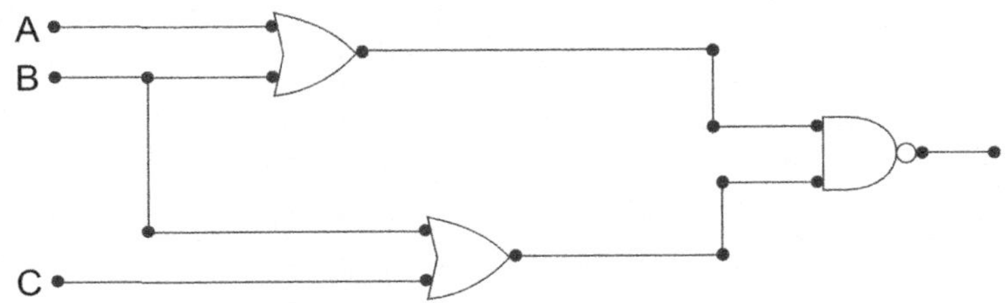

Solution:

$\overline{(A + B).(B + C)}$

39. Translate into Boolean expression.

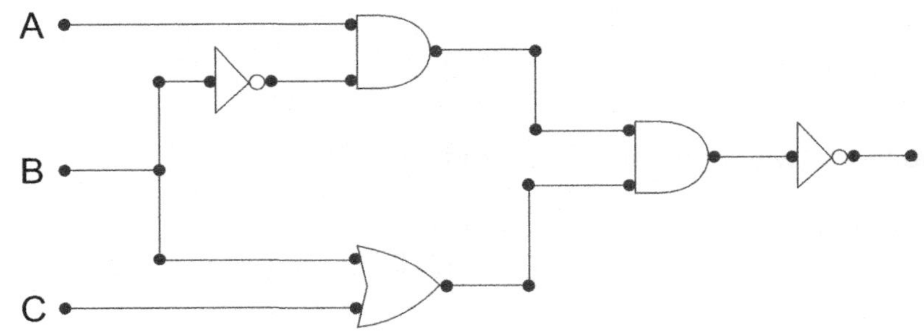

Solution:

$\overline{(A.\overline{B}).(B + C)}$

40. Translate the logic gate in Boolean expression.

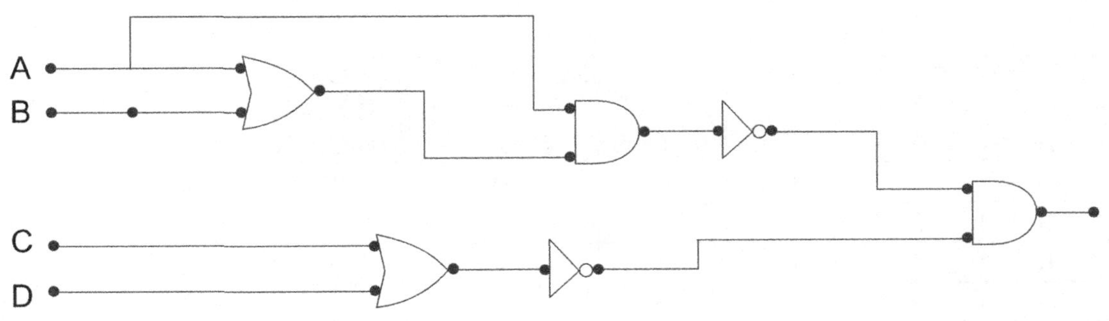

Solution:

$\overline{((A + B).A)}.\overline{(C + D)}$

41. Simplify using truth table.

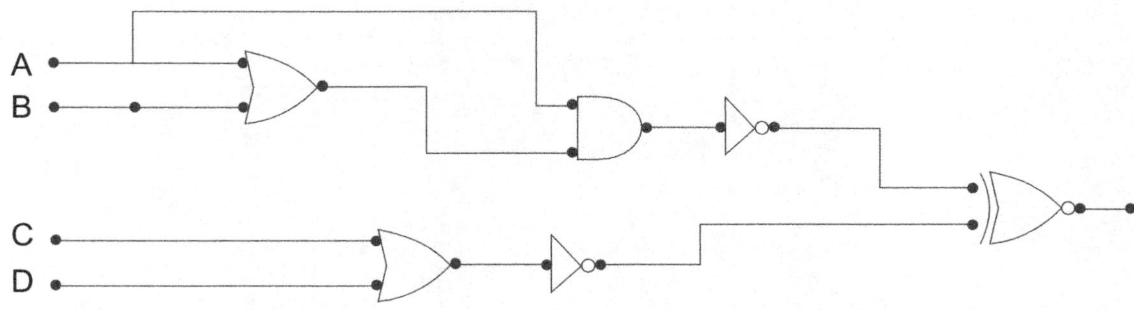

Solution:

$((A + B).A) \overline{\oplus} (\bar{C}.\bar{D})$

A	B	C	D	A OR B	A AND (A OR B)	NOT (A AND (A OR B))	NOT(C OR D)	NOT (A AND (A OR B)) XNOR NOT(C OR D)
0	0	0	0	0	0	1	1	1
0	0	0	1	0	0	1	0	0
0	0	1	0	0	0	1	0	0
0	0	1	1	0	0	1	0	0
0	1	0	0	1	0	1	1	1
0	1	0	1	1	0	1	0	0
0	1	1	0	1	0	1	0	0
0	1	1	1	1	0	1	0	0
1	0	0	0	0	0	1	1	1
1	0	0	1	0	0	1	0	0
1	0	1	0	0	0	1	0	0
1	0	1	1	0	0	1	0	0
1	1	0	0	1	1	0	1	0
1	1	0	1	1	1	0	0	1
1	1	1	0	1	1	0	0	1
1	1	1	1	1	1	0	0	1

42. Translate into Boolean expression.

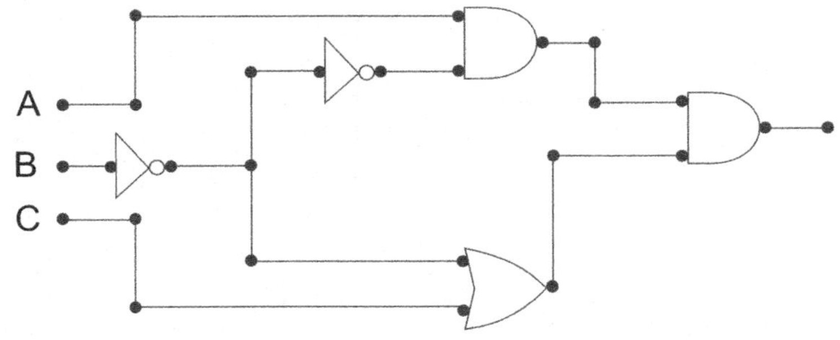

Solution:

$(A.B).(\overline{B} + C)$

43. Simplify using truth table.

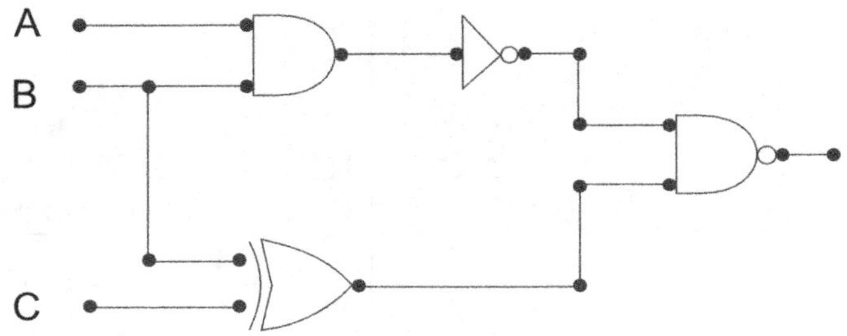

Solution:

$(A.B).(\overline{B \oplus C})$

A	B	C	NOT(A AND B)	B XOR C	NOT(A AND B) NAND (B XOR C)
0	0	0	1	0	1
0	0	1	1	1	0
0	1	0	1	1	0
0	1	1	1	0	1
1	0	0	1	0	1
1	0	1	1	1	0
1	1	0	0	1	1
1	1	1	0	0	1

44. Translate into Boolean expression.

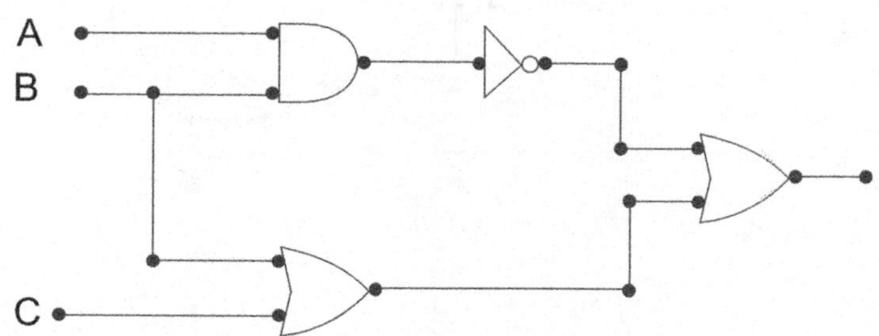

Solution:

$\overline{(A.B)} + (B + C)$

45. Simplify using truth table.

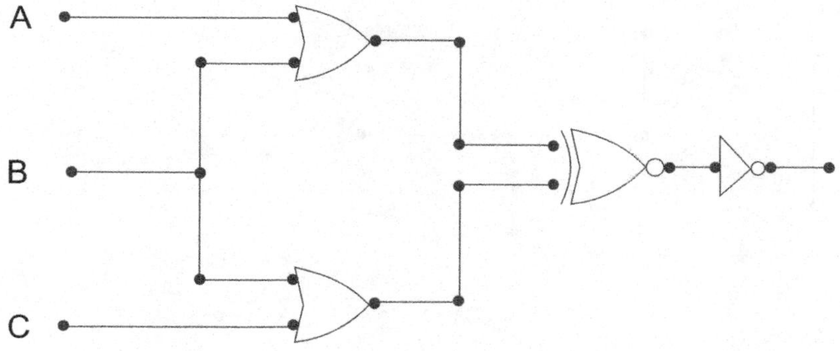

Solution:

$(A + B) \oplus (B + C)$

A	B	C	A OR B	B OR C	(A OR B) XOR (B OR C
0	0	0	0	0	0
0	0	1	0	1	1
0	1	0	1	1	0
0	1	1	1	1	0
1	0	0	1	0	1
1	0	1	1	1	0
1	1	0	1	1	0
1	1	1	1	1	0

46. Translate the following into Boolean expression.

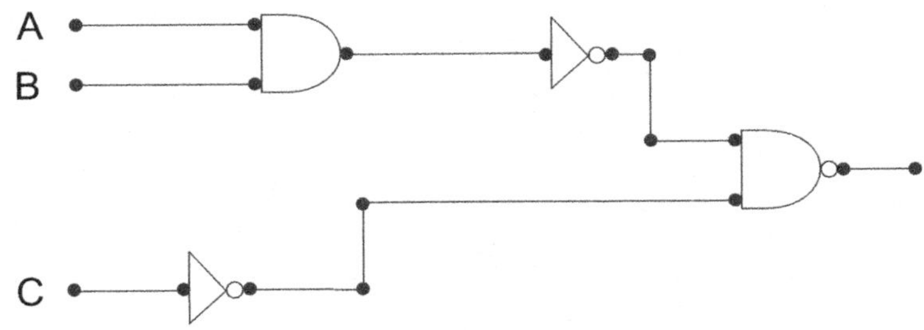

Solution:

$\overline{\overline{(A.B)}.\overline{C}} = (A.B).C$

47. Simplify using truth table.

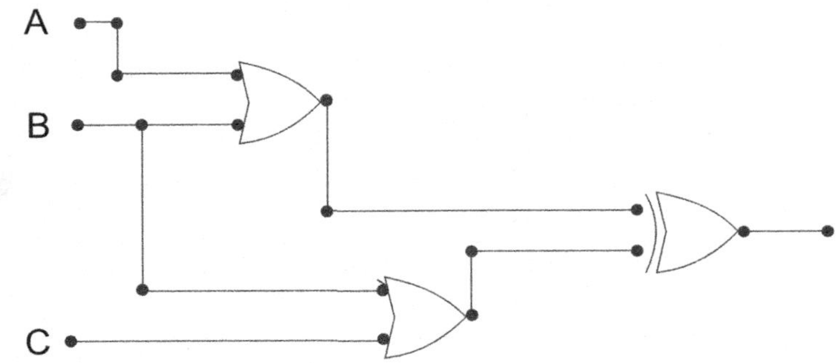

Solution:

$(A + B) \oplus (B + C)$

A	B	C	A OR B	B OR C	(A OR B) XOR (B OR C)
0	0	0	0	0	0
0	0	1	0	1	1
0	1	0	1	1	0
0	1	1	1	1	0
1	0	0	1	0	1
1	0	1	1	1	0
1	1	0	1	1	0
1	1	1	1	1	0

48. Simplify using truth table.

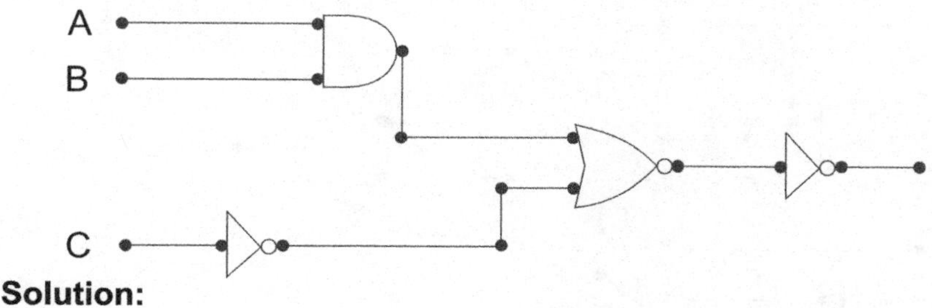

Solution:

$(A.B) + \overline{C}$

A	B	C	A AND B	A AND B OR NOT C
0	0	0	0	1
0	0	1	0	0
0	1	0	0	1
0	1	1	0	0
1	0	0	0	1
1	0	1	0	0
1	1	0	1	1
1	1	1	1	1

49. Translate the following into Boolean expression.

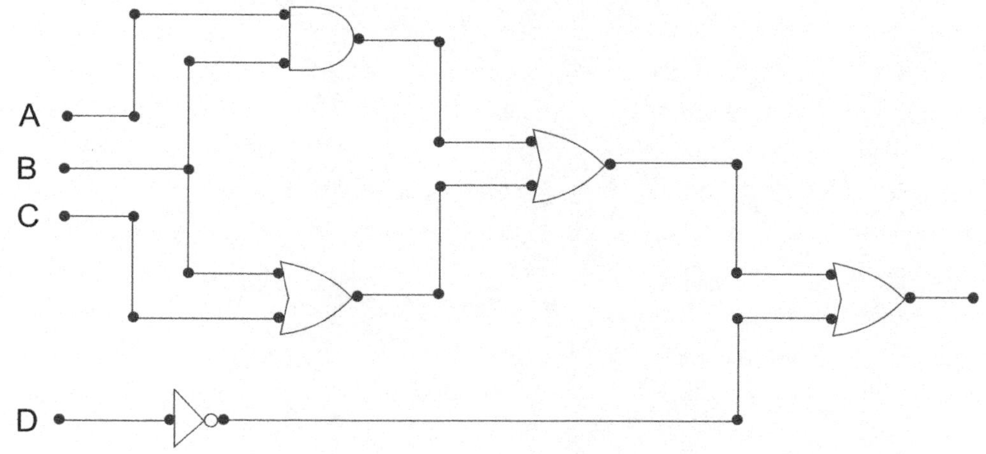

Solution:

$\overline{(A.B) + (B + C)} + \overline{D}$

50. Translate into Boolean expression.

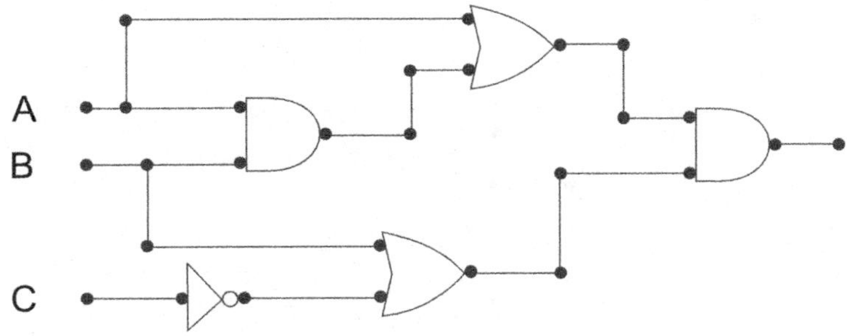

Solution:

$((A.B) + A).(B + \overline{C})$

1) What is the output of the below program?

```
B = "BANANASBANANASBANANAS"
T = "" : U = "" : V = "": W = ""
for I = len(B) – 1 to 0 step -1
 T[I:I] = T[I:I] + B [I:I]
Next I
END
for I = 0 to len(B) – 1
  IF T[I:I] = "A"
    THEN U = U + T[I:I]
  ELSEIF T[I:I] = "N"
     V[I:I] = V[I:I] + T[I:I]
  ELSE
    W[I:I] = W[I:I] + T[I:I]
  END
next I
PRINT U
PRINT V
PRINT W
END
```

Output :

```
AAAAAAAAA
NNNNNN
BSBSBS
```

2) What is the output of the below program?

```
B = "LETITSNOWLETITSNOW"
T = "" : U = "" : V = "": W = ""
for I = len(B) – 1 to 0 step -1
 T[I:I] = T[I:I] + B [I:I]
Next I
END
for I = 0 to len(B) – 1
  IF T[I:I] = "L" OR T[I:I] = "E" OR T[I:I] = "T"
    THEN U[I:I] = U[I:I] + T[I:I]
  ELSE
     V[I:I] = V[I:I] + T[I:I]
 END
next I
PRINT U
PRINT V
END
```

Output :

```
LETTLETT
ISNOWISNOW
```

3) What is the output of the below program?

```
B = "GOGREENSAVEEARTH"
T = "" : U = "" : V = "": W = ""
for I = len(B) – 1 to 0 step -1
 T[I:I] = T[I:I] + B [I:I]
Next I
END
for I = 0 to len(B) – 1
  IF T[I:I] = "A" OR T[I:I] = "E" OR T[I:I] = "O"
    THEN U[I:I] = U[I:I] + T[I:I]
  ELSE
    V[I:I] = V[I:I] + T[I:I]
 END
next I
PRINT U
PRINT LEN[U]
PRINT V
PRINT LEN[V]
END
```

Output :

```
OEEAEEA
7
GGRNSVRTH
9
```

4) What is the output of the below program?

```
B = "YENOMONEY"
T = "" : U = "" : V = "": W = ""
for I = len(B) – 1 to 0 step -1
 T[I:I] = T[I:I] + B [I:I]
Next I
END
for I = 0 to len(B) – 1
  IF T[I:I] = "E" OR T[I:I] = "O"
    THEN U[I:I] = U[I:I] + T[I:I]
  ELSE
    V[I:I] = V[I:I] + T[I:I]
  END
 NEXT I
PRINT U
PRINT LEN[U]
PRINT V
PRINT LEN[V]
END
```

Output :

```
YNMNY
5
EOOE
4
```

5) What is the output of the below program?

```
char line [100]
int v ,u
i = "enter the string"
for (int i = 0; line[I] !='\0'; ++i)
{
 if (line[i] == 'a' || line[i] == 'e' || line [i] == 'i' || line[i] == 'o' || line[i] == 'u')
++v
else
++u
}
PRINT v
PRINT u
end
```

Output :

4
12

6) What is the output of the below program?

```
X = ""
Y = ""
string firstname = "Weasley"
string lastname = "Manny"
string fullname = firstname + lastname
fullname += "Jr"
string fullname += '.'

  FOR I= 0 TO LEN [fullname] – 1

        X[I:I]  = X[I:I] + fullname

     NEXT I
  END
  FOR I= 0 TO LEN [X] – 1
        IF (X[I:I] !=  "E") AND (X[I:I] != "A")

        THEN Y[I:I] = X[I:I] + Y[I:I]
        NEXT I
        END
     PRINT Y
END
```

Output :

WslyMnnyJr.

7) What is the output of the below program?

```
X[I:I]  = "REDROOTPUTUPTOORDER"
T = "" : U = "" : V = "": W = ""
for I = len(B)  – 1 to  0 step -1
  T[I:I] = T[I:I] +X [I:I]
Next I
END
for I = 0 to len( T) – 1
   IF T[I:I] = "E" OR T[I:I] = "O" OR T[I:I] = "U"
     THEN U[I:I]  = U[I:I]  + T[I:I]
   ELSE
      V[I:I]  = V[I:I]  + T[I:I]
   END
 next I
  PRINT U
  PRINT LEN[U]
  PRINT V
  PRINT LEN[V]
END
```

Output :

RDRTPTPTRDR
11
EOOUUOOE
8

8) What is the output of the below program?

```
char line[100]
int v,c,d
i = "ihave54codesrunning"
for (int i = 0; line[I] !='\0'; ++i)
{
 if (line[i] == 'a' || line[i] == 'e' || line[i] == 'i' || line[i] == 'o' || line[i] == 'u')
++v
elseif (line[i] = '0' && line[i] <= '9')
++d
else
++c
}
Display v
Display c
Display d
```

Output :

7
10
2

9) What is the output of the below program?

```
T = "RACECARRACECAR"
U = "" : V = ""
for I = 0 to len(B) – 1
  IF T[I:I] = "A" OR T[I:I] = "R"
    THEN U[I:I]  = U[I:I]  + T[I:I]
  ELSE
     V[I:I]  = V[I:I]  + T[I:I]
 END
next I
PRINT U
PRINT V
END
```

Output :

RAARRAAR
CECCEC

10) What is the output of the below program?

```
X = ""
Y = ""
string firstname = "JIMMY"
string lastname = "POTTER"
string fullname = firstname + lastname
fullname += "JRJR"
string fullname += '.'

 FOR I= 0 TO LEN [X] – 1

        X [I:I] = X[I:I] +  fullname
       NEXT I
 END
 FOR I= 0 TO LEN [X[I:I]] – 1
        IF (X[I:I] !=  "E") OR (X[I:I] != "I" OR (X[I:I] != "O")
        THEN Y[I:I] = X[I:I] + Y[I:I]
         NEXT I
       END
 PRINT Y[I:I]
 PRINT LEN[Y[I:I]]
END
```

Output :

JMMYPTTR
8

11) What is the output of the below program?

```
X = "ROSSHASGONETOVEGAS"

Y= “”
for I = len(X)  – 1 to  0 step -1
  Y[I:I] = Y + X [I:I]
Next I
PRINT Y
END
```

Output :

SAGEVOTENOGSAHSSOR

12) What is the output of the below program?

```
string line
 X[I:I] = ”@ASANTA@ 12&%ATNASA@”
 Y[I:I] = "" : Z[I:I] = ""
for I = len(X)  – 1 to  0 step -1
  Y[I:I] = Y[I:I] + X[I:I]
  Next I
End
for I =  0 to len(Y)  – 1  step 1
   IF  Y[I:I] >= A TO Y[I:I] <= Z
    THEN Z[I:I] = Z[I:I] + Y[I:I]
   NEXT
PRINT Z
END
```

Output :

ASANTAATNASA

13) What is the output of the below program?

```
X[I:I] = "PLASMATELIVISION"
Y = "": Y = "": U = "": T = ""

For I = 0 TO len(X) – 1 step 1
    IF  X[I:I] = "A" OR  X[I:I] = "E" OR  X[I:I] = "I" OR  X[I:I] = "O"
        THEN Z[I:I] = Z[I:I] + Y[I:I]
    ELSEIF
        U[I:I] = U[I:I] + Y[I:I]
    END
NEXT I
  T = U[I:I] + Z[I:I]
        PRINT T
        PRINT LEN[T]
        END
```

Output :

PLSMTLVSNAAEIIIO
16

14) What is the output of the below program?

```
char line [100]
int v
i = "COMPUTATION"
for (int i = 0; line[I] !='\0'; ++i)
{
 if (line[i] == 'C' || line [i] == 'O' || line[i] == 'T' || line[i] == 'N' || line[i] == 'A')
++v
else
display "Error"
}
Display v
```

Output :

6

15) What is the output of the below program?

```
B = "ANNAANNA"
NUM = 0
T = ""
for I = len(B) – 1 to 0 step -1
T = T + B [I:I]
Next I
end
for I = 0 to len(B) – 1
If A[I:I] == T[I:I] then NUM = NUM + 1
next I
end
print NUM
```

Output :

8

16) What is the output of the below program?

```
string firstname = "Saam"
string lastname = "SeverrusSnnap"
string fullname = firstname + lastname
N = "":
M = ""
A[I:I] = string fullname
FOR i = 0 TO LEN[A] - 1
      IF A[I:I] != A[I+1: I+1] THEN
         N = N + A[I:I]
      NEXT I
END
FOR I = 0 TO LEN[N] - 1
   IF N[I:I] > "B"
     THEN M[I:I] = M[I:I] + N[I:I]
   NEXT I
PRINT M
END
```

Output :

SmSeverusSnp

17) What is the output of the below program?

```
string line
line = "CcOmputer"
for (int i =0; i< line.size(); ++i)
if (!((line[i] >= 'a' && line[i] <= 'z') || (line[i] >= 'A' && line[i] <= 'Z')))
line[i]='\0'
display line
```

Output:

cmputerC

18) What is the output of the below program?

```
N = ""
string sentence = "MONTREALINCANADA"
s = sentence.insert(9, " IS ")
FOR I = 0 TO LEN[N] – 1
IF S[I:I] > "E"
  THEN M = M + N[I: I]
  NEXT I
 PRINT LEN[M]
END
```

Output:

MontrlisinCn

19) What is the output of the below program?

```
char line[100]
int v,c,d
i = "route 67"
for (int i = 0; line[I] !='\0'; ++i)
{
 if (line[i] == 'a' || line [i] == 'e' || line[i] == 'i' || line[i] == 'o' || line[i] == 'u')
++v
elseif (line[i] >= '0' && line[i] <= '9')
++d
else
++c
}
Display v
Display c
Display d
```

Output:

3
3
2

20) What is the output of the below program?

```
str = "SCOOTERPARK"
int c = 0;
For i = 0 to len[str]-1
  c = c + len[str[i:i]]
display c
```

Output:

11

21) What is the output of the below program?

```
string line
line = "l1kel1h00d"
N = ""
for (int i = 0; i < line.size(); ++i)
  for i = 0 to len[line] - 1
    if (!((line[i] >= 'a' && line[i] <= 'z') || (line[i] >= 'A' && line[i] <= 'Z')))
   N = N + line[i,j]
   next
  end
next
PRINT N
PRINT len[N]
end
```

Output:

lkelhd

6

22) What is the output of the below program?

```
char line [100]
N = ''''
line = "notebook"
for (i = 0 to len[line] - 1)
{
 if (line[i,j] == 'a' || line [i,j] == 'e' || line[i,j] == 'i' || line[i,j] == 'o' || line[i,j] == 'u')
 then N = N + line[i,j]
}
next i
  PRINT len[N]
end
```

Output

4

23) What is the output of the below program?

```
B = "madammillermadam"
NUM = 0
T = ""
S = ""
For i = len(B) – 1 to  0 step -1
 if B[i:i] > "e"
     then T = T + B [i:i]
Next i
For i = 0 to len(T) – 1
If T[i:i] != "m"
     then S = S + T[i:i]
next i
PRINT S
PRINT len[S]
```

Output:

illr
4

24) What is the output of the below program?

```
string line
line = "Aerop12nE"
for (int i =0; i< line.size(); ++i)
  if (!((line[i] >= 'a' && line[i] <= 'z') || (line[i] >= 'A' && line[i] <= 'Z')))
   next
 PRINT line
end
```

Output:

AeropnE

25) What is the output of the below program?

```
line = "p2.'67reep2weep"
for (int i = 0; i < line.size(); ++i)
if (!((line[i] >= 'a' && line[i] <= 'z') || (line[i] >= 'A' && line[i] <= 'Z')))
line[i] ='\0'
display line
```

Output :

preepweep

26) What is the output of the below program?

```
char line[100]
int v,c,d
i = "34 rue sherbrooke"
for (int i = 0; line[I]!='\0'; ++i)
{
 if (line[i] == 'a' || line [i] == 'e' || line[i] == 'i' || line[i] == 'o' || line[i] == 'u')
++v
elseif (line[i] = '0' && line[i] <= '9')
++d
else
++c
}
Display v
Display c
Display d
```

Output:

6
9
2

27) What is the output of the below program?

```
X = "NOELSEESLEON"
NUM=0
T = ""
S = ""
For i = len(X) – 1 to  0 step -1
  if X[i:i] > "d"
      then T = T + B [i:i]
Next i
For i = 0 to len(T) – 1
    If T[i:i] != "N"
      then S = S + T[i:i]
  next i
PRINT S
PRINT len[S]
end
```

Output :

OELSEESLEO
10

28) What is the output of the below program?

```
char line [100]
V = ""
U = ""
X = "dataanalyticsanalyticsanalyticsdata"
FOR I = 0 TO LEN[X] – 1
IF X[I: I] = "a" or X[I: I] = "e" or X[I: I] = "i" or X[I: I] = "o" or X[I: I] = "u"
  THEN V = V + X[I: I]
ELSE
    U = U + X[I: I]
NEXT I
PRINT "V = " V
PRINT "LV = " LEN[V]
PRINT "U = " U
PRINT "LU = " LEN[U]
```

Output:

V = aaaaiaaiaaiaa
LV = 13
U = dtnlytcsnlytcsnlytcsta
LV = 22

29) What is the output of the below program?

```
string firstname = "SAAMM"
string middlename = "PPOOEETRRYY"
string lastname = " POOTTERPOETRRY "
string Initial = "MRR."
string fullname = Initial + middlename + firstname + lastname
 N= "":
 M= ""
 A[i,j] = string fullname
 FOR i = 0 TO LEN[A]  – 1
                          IF A[I:I] != A[I + 1: I + 1] THEN
 N = N + A[I:I]
 NEXT I
 FOR I = 0 TO LEN[N]  – 1
 IF (N[I:I] > "C" THEN M = M + N[I:I]
 NEXT I
 PRINT fullname
 PRINT N
 PRINT M
 END
```

Output

MRR.SAAMMPPOOEETRRYYPOOTTERPOETRRY
MRSMPOETRYPOTERPOETRY
21

30) What is the output of the below program?

```
string line
line = "aBSsD./W\POOK"
for (int i = 0; i < line.size(); ++i)
if (!((line[i] >= 'a' && line[i] <= 'z') || (line[i] >= 'A' && line[i] <= 'Z')))
line[i] = '\0'
display line
```

Output :

aBSsDWPOK

31) What is the output of the below program?

```
B = "CRAZYR00MROOM50921NUMBER770001008"
T = ""
S = ""
U = ""
V = ""
For I = len(B) – 1 to  0 step -1
 if B[I:I] >= "A" || [I:I] >= "0"
      then T = T + B [I:I]
Next I
For i = 0 to len(T) – 1
If T[I:I] = "A" or T[I:I] = "E" or T[I:I] = "I" or T[I:I] = "O" or T[I:I] = "U"
      then S = S + T[I:I]
else if T[I:I] >= 0 and T[I:I] <= 9
      then U =  U + T[I:I]
else
     V = V + T[I:I]
next i
PRINT S
PRINT "LS = " len[S]
PRINT "U = " U
PRINT "LU = " len[U]
PRINT V
PRINT "LV = " len[V]
end
```

Output :

S = AOOUE
LS = 5
U = 0050921770001008
LU = 16
V = CRZYRMRMNMBR
LV = 12

32) What is the output of the below program?

```
A = "THEUSAINNORTHAMERICA"
B = "THEAMERICANCONTINENT"
X = “”
Y = ""
FOR I = 0 TO LEN[A] – 1
IF A[I: I] < B[I: I]
  THEN X[I:I] = X[I:I] + A[I:I]
ELSE  X[I:I] = X[I:I] + B[I:I]
NEXT I
FOR I = 0 TO LEN[X] – 1
  IF X[I: I] > “D” THEN Y = Y + X[I: I]
NEXT I
  PRINT " X = " X
  PRINT " Y = " Y
  PRINT "Length (Y) = " LEN[Y]
END
```

Output :

X = THEAMAIICANCHAMENECA

Y = THEMIINHMENE

Length (Y) = 12

33) What is the output of the below program?

```
string line
line = ”OOutput OString701”
for (int i = 0; i< line.size(); ++i)
if (!((line[i] >= ‘a’ && line[i] <= ’z’) | | (line[i] >= ‘A’ && line[i] <= ’Z’)))
line[i]=’\0’
display line
```

Output :

OutputString

34) What is the output of the below program?

```
X = “CCOOOMPUTTTINNGNUUMBERRSS”
Y = ""
Z = ""
FOR I = 0 TO LEN[X] – 1
IF X[I:I] > “E” THEN Y = Y + X[I:I]
   Z = Z + len[Y]
NEXT I
   PRINT "Y = "  Y
   PRINT "Length (Y) = " Z
END
```

Output :

Y = OOOMPUTTTINNGNUUMBRRSS
Length (Y) = 22

35) What is the output of the below program?

```
B = ”001DATAMINNINGGINMILLEANNIUM2020”
T = “”
S = ""
U = ""
V = ""
For I = len(B) – 1 to  0 step -1
 if B[I:I] >= "A"  | |  B[I:I] >= "0"
      then T[I:I] = T[I:I] + B[I:I]
Next i
end
For I = len(T) – 1 to 0
    If T[I:I] = "A" or T[I:I] = "E" or T[I:I] = "I" or T[I:I] = "O" or T[I:I] = "U"
      then S = S + T[I:I]
    else if T[I:I] >= 0 and T[I:I] <= 9
      then U =  U + T[I:I]
    else
      V = V + T[I:I]
 next i
   PRINT S
   PRINT "LS = " len[S]
  PRINT "U = " U
  PRINT "LU = " len[U]
  PRINT V
  PRINT "LV = " len[V]
end
```

Output:

DATAMINNINGGINMILLEANNIU
S = AAIIIIEAIU
LS = 10
U = 0012020
LU = 7
V = DTMNNNGGNMLLNNM
LV = 15

36) What is the output of the below program?

```
X = "22222BLUEBERRYAND33333APPLEBERRIES"
T = ""
S = ""
U = ""
V = ""
For I = len(X) – 1 to  0 step -1
 if X[I:I] >= "A" || X[I:I] >= "0"
      then T[I:I]  = T[I:I] + X[I:I]
Next I
For I = 0 to len(T) – 1
If T[I:I] = "A" or T[I:I] = "E" or T[I:I] = "I" or T[I:I] = "O" or T[I:I] = "U"
      then S = S + T[I:I]
else if T[I:I] >= 0 and T[I:I] <= 9
      then U =  U + T[I:I]
else
     V = V + T[I:I]
next I
PRINT S
PRINT "LS = " len[S]
PRINT "U = " U
PRINT "LU = " len[U]
PRINT V
PRINT "LV = " len[V]
end
```

Output :

22222BLUEBERRYAND33333APPLEBERRIESCRATES
S = UEEAAEEIEAE
LS = 11
U = 2222233333
LU = 10
V = BLBRRYNDPPLBRRSCRTS
LV = 19

37) What is the output of the below program?

```
string line
line = "OutpU.tstri7g"
for (int i =0; i< line.size(); ++i)
if (!((line[i] >= 'a' && line[i] <= 'z') || (line[i] >= 'A' && line[i] <= 'Z')))
line[i]='\0'
display line
```

Output :

utpUtstrig

38) What is the output of the below program?

```
char line[100]
int v,c,d
line = "actualement"
for (int i = 0; line[I]! ='\0'; ++i)
{
 if (line[i] == 'a' || line [i] == 'e' || line[i] == 'i' || line[i] == 'o' || line[i] == 'u')
++v
elseif (line[i] = '0' && line[i] <= '9')
++d
else
++c
}
Display v
Display c
Display d
```

Output :

5
6
0

39) What is the output of the below program?

```
string line
line = "23He11HeA7en"
for (int i = 0; i < line.size(); ++i)
if (!((line[i] >= 'a' && line[i] <= 'z') || (line[i] >= 'A' && line[i] <= 'Z')))
line[i]='\0'
display line
```

Output

HeHeAen

40) What is the output of the below program?

```
A = "KAY AKK AYA KIN  GKAY AKIN "
B = "KIT  EKO TEK  ETO KITE  KOTE"
X = ""
Y = ""
FOR I = 0 TO LEN[A] – 1
IF A[I:I] < B[I:I]
THEN X[I:I] = X[I:I] + A[I:I]
ELSE  X[I:I] = X[I:I] + B[I:I]
NEXT I
FOR I = 0 TO LEN[N] – 1
IF X[I: I] > "D" THEN Y[I:I] = Y[I:I] + X[I: I]
NEXT I
PRINT ' X = '  X
PRINT ' Y = '  Y
PRINT ' Length (Y) = ' LEN[Y]
END
```

Output

X = KAT AKK AEA EIA GIAE AKIE
Y = KTKKEAEIGIEKIE
Length (Y) = 14

41) What is the output of the below program?

```
X = "STRINGYSTRINGSTRINGYSTRINGE"
Y = ""
Z = ""
For I = 0  to len(X) – 1
  if X[I:I] != "S"
       then Y = Y + X[I:I]
   else
       Z = Z+X[I:I]
Next I
PRINT ' Y = '  Z
PRINT ' Z = '  Z
PRINT 'Length = ' len[Y]
end
```

Output:

Y = TRINGYTRINGTRINGYTRINGE
Z = SSSS
Length = 23

42) What is the output of the below program if the user entered "Lauren"?

```
X = "NOLEMON,NOMELON,NOLEMON,NOMELON"
T = ""
For I = len(X) – 1 to  0 step -1
 if X[I:I] >= "A" OR X[I:I] = ","
      then T[I:I] = T[I:I] + X[I:I]
Next I
PRINT 'T = ' T
PRINT "LT = " len[T]
end
```

Output:

T = NOLEMON,NOMELON,NOLEMON,NOMELON
LT = 31

43) What is the output of the below program?

```
X = "NOMISTSORFROSTSIMON"
T = ""
For I = len(X) – 1 to  0 step -1
 if X[I:I] >= "A" OR X[I:I] = ","
     then T[I:I]  = T[I:I] + X [I:I]
 Next I
PRINT 'T = ' T
PRINT "LT = " len[T]
end
```

Output:

T = NOMISTSORFROSTSIMON
LT = 19

44) What is the output of the below program?

```
X = "MERRYANDBRIGHTJOYTOTHEWORLD"
T = ""
U = ""
For I = 0 to len(X) – 1 step 1
 if X[I:I] = "A" OR X[I:I] = "E" OR X[I:I] = "O"
     then T[I:I] = T[I:I] + X[I:I]
  else
 U[I:I] = U[I:I] + X[I:I]
Next I
  PRINT 'T = ' T
  PRINT "LT = " len[T]
  PRINT 'U = ' U
  PRINT "LU = " len[U]
end
```

Output:

T = MRRYNDBRIGHTJYTTHEWRLD
LT = 22
U = AOOO
UT = 4

45) What is the output of the below program?

```
X = "NATUREISWRITTENINMATHEMATICALLANGUAGE"
T = ""
U = ""
For I = 0 to len(X) – 1 step 1
  if X[I:I] < S
    then T[I:I] = T[I:I] + X[I:I]
  else
    U[I:I] = U[I:I] + X[I:I]
  Next I
    PRINT 'T = ' T
    PRINT "LT = " len[T]
    PRINT 'U = ' U
    PRINT "LU = " len[U]
  end
end
```

Output:

T = NAREIRIENINMAHEMAICALLANGAGE
LT = 28
U = TUSWTTTTU
LU = 9

46) What is the output of the below program if the user entered "Noah"?

```
string name = "Neel"
input string uname
while (true)
if uname == name
display "Same name"
else
display "Different name"
```

Output :

Different name

47) What is the output of the below program?

```
X = "TENDIPARAPIDNET"
Y = "": Z = "": T = "" : U = ""
FOR I = 0 TO LEN [X] - 2
                    Y[I:I] = X[I:I]+ Y[I:I]
          NEXT I
END
FOR I = 0 TO LEN [Y] - 2 STEP 2
        IF  Y[I:I] <  Y[I + 1:I + 1]
          THEN
              T[I:I] = T[I:I] + Y[I + 1: I + 1]
         ELSE
              U[I:I] = U[I:I] + Y[I:I]
         END IF
        NEXT I
  Z[I:I] = Z[I:I] + T[I:I] + U[I:I]
  PRINT Y
  PRINT Z
END
```

Output:

Y = ENDIPARAPIDNET
T= NIDE
U= PRP
Z = NIDEPRP

48) What is the output of the below program?

```
X = "JOYTOTHEWORLD"
Y = "": Z = ""
FOR i = LEN [X] - 2 TO 0
        Y = X[i : i] + Y
    NEXT i
  IF Y != "O" OR Y != "A" OR Y != "E"
        THEN Z = Z + Y
  ENDIF
PRINT Y
PRINT Z
END
```

Output:

Y = ROWEHTOTYOJ
Z = RWHTTYJ

49) What is the output of the below program? what are the unique letters?

```
X = "SLEDGEISDASHINGTHROUGHTHESNOW"
Y = "": Z = ""
FOR i = 7 TO LEN [X] - 1
        Y = X[i:i] + Y
    NEXT i
  IF Y != "O" OR Y != "A" OR Y != "H" OR Y!= "D"
      THEN Z = Z + Y
  ENDIF
PRINT Y
PRINT Z
END
```

Output:

Y = ISDASHINGTHROUGHTHESNOW

Z = ISSINGTRUGTESNW

unique letters are : ' I' , 'S' , 'N', 'G', 'T','R' , 'U' ,'E' 'W'

50) What is the output of the below program?

```
S = "ROTATORROTATORROTATORS"
Z = 0
X = "": Y = ""
For I = len(B) – 1 to  0 step -1
    X[I:I] = X[I:I] + S[I:I]
Next I
For I = 1 to len(B) – 1
  If S[I:I] == X[I:I]
    Y[I:I] = Y[I:I] + X[I:I]
   then Z[I:I] = Z[I:I] + Len[Y]
 next I
  PRINT " X = "  X
  PRINT " Y = "  Y
  PRINT "Length = " len[Y]
```

Output :

X = SROTATORROTATORROTATOR

Y = ROTATORROTATORROTATOR

Length = 21

Made in the USA
Coppell, TX
05 February 2024